*Conversations With a Pedophile*

# Conversations With a Pedophile

## *In the interest of our children*

## DR. AMY HAMMEL-ZABIN

Fort Lee | New Jersey

Published by Barricade Books Inc.
185 Bridge Plaza North
Suite 308-A
Fort Lee, NJ 07024

www.barricadebooks.com

Library of Congress Cataloging-in-Publication Data

Hammel-Zabin, Amy.
    Conversations with a pedophile / Amy Hammel-Zabin.
        p. cm.
    ISBN 1-56980-247-5
    1. Pedophilia--United States--Case Studies. 2. Child molesters--
United States--Interviews. 3. Child sexual abuse--Prevention. I. Title.

HQ72.U53H338  2003
306.77--dc21
                                                        2003040413
Manufactured in the United States of America
First Printing

# DEDICATION

To my children Benjamin and Alixandra,
I am blessed to be your mother.

# Contents

# A Personal Note

It's important to know that the typical pedophile is not the stereotypical "stranger in the bushes," wearing a trench coat and offering candy. The typical child molester is your neighbor, your clergyman, the local scoutmaster, your babysitter; he or she may even be your friend or your relative. The pedophile hides in plain sight—goes to work, attends church services, and participates in community activities. Providing, of course, those activities give him or her access to your kids.

There are few crimes more horrifying to contemplate than the sexual assault of a child. Any mention of the subject awakens feelings of repulsion, rage, fear, and disbelief. We all share those feelings. Even among criminal offenders, the child molester is considered a sewer rat in the social hierarchy. Among parents, the need to protect children from sexual abusers has led to legislation such as Megan's Law. Among educators, awareness of childhood sexual abuse has spawned many controversial programs that attempt to educate the very young about "good touching" and "bad touching."

Yet as a society, our attitudes toward childhood sexual abuse warrant scrutiny. Why don't we feel as great a need to warn our communities as when a murderer or rapist is released from prison? As much as we may want to protect our children from sexual abuse—and for all our good intentions—the fact is that most of us are ignorant of how and why such crimes come about. Though recent decades have seen break-throughs in contemporary attitudes about acceptable sexual conduct, most people still regard pedophilia as a behavioral phenomenon too horrific to attempt to understand.

Unless the unimaginable happens to someone they know. Until then, childhood sexual abuse is something that, as parents and as a concerned society, we are content to keep at arm's length. Sexual abuse is something we want desperately to believe happens only to somebody else—to someone else's daughter, or the neighbor's boy, or the family down the street. We teach our kids not to talk to strangers, and believe that this is enough to keep them safe. Yet to believe that abuse only happens at the hands of "strangers" is to put your children at grave risk.

I know, because as a music therapist I have worked with child molesters and the abused for much of my career. I know, because I was a victim of childhood sexual abuse.

As much as we comfort ourselves with the notion that children are better protected in today's society than ever before, they are not. Even though modern parenting methods call for greater involvement in our children's activities, increased adult supervision, and improved family communication, the incidence of childhood sexual abuse is on the rise.

We cannot afford to ignore the truth any longer. Current estimates of the incidence of sexual abuse of girls range from 25 percent to 38 percent. The abuse of boys is considered by researchers to be consistently underreported; some have estimated it to be as high as 17 — 25 percent. Many studies use figures that only reflect reported cases. The FBI and the Justice Department have determined that only one in ten cases is actually reported, while other researchers postulate that approximately one-third of all abuse victims keep secret their sexual abuse and carry a terrible psychological legacy into adulthood. Most importantly, 75 percent to 95 percent of the offenders, regardless of the victim's sex, *are known by and may be related to the child.*

Since sexual abuse typically occurs at the hands of a known, trusted individual, it introduces a sense of danger in what ought to be a child's safe world. This invasion is the most damaging aspect of abuse because it destroys the child's trust in his or her own feelings and instincts. This results in a sense of alienation, a feeling of "differentness." The child who feels like a stranger to himself also loses confidence, ability to make ordinary social contact, and happy childhood memories. This child has an incapacity to play, to learn, and to accept normal, loving nurturing. People with a history of abuse are plagued by anxiety and depression well into adulthood because they generally believe that events are beyond their control. Worse still, they can go on to abuse others when they grow up.

Clearly, the pedophile must be stopped, but we can't stop what we don't understand. Knowing that a real relationship exists between the victim and the offender is essential to understanding the child molester. Sexuality is commonly thought to be the major ingredient of this relationship. Actually the dominant element is control.

As a child, I never understood the nature of the victim-abuser relationship, though I had been regularly and systematically abused by my father and paternal grandfather. I never understood how I was selected as a victim or why I kept my terrible secret for so long. It wasn't until I began the work with the man whom I call "Alan" in these pages that I began to be liberated from the darkness surrounding the awful reality of my past. He, more than anyone else I had ever encountered in my work, helped me finally understand the planning and methods of the child molester, and the carefully controlled web of lies he used to ensnare hundreds of innocent children.

This book is the story of a unique relationship. I originally served as Alan's music therapist after he was incarcerated, but it was through our subsequent correspondence, spanning an entire decade, that he shared with me the insights that he gained as a result of our work together. Finally, getting inside the mind of an offender and understanding his madness was crucial to my coming to terms with having been a victim. The result has been a profoundly healing experience.

In telling the story of the incredible dynamic between us, I hope to provide the reader access to this kind of understanding in a way that is not only informative but also deeply affecting. As much as most people may fear the pedophile, they know almost nothing about the inner workings of his mind. There has never been a comprehensive study of the motivations and psychology of a child molester. As a society, we know that such people exist, but we do not understand why.

This book seeks to address that deficit.

# Acknowledgements

There are three people in my life without whose presence this book would not have been possible. My mother, despite all obstacles, who has always been an example of strength and creativity. My mainstay, Marty Goldray, who helped me place a level of importance on both myself and my work. And my prince, my husband Steve, without whom I couldn't live my enchanted life. It was worth all I experienced as a child in order to share our incredible family together.

There are also exquisite personal friends and colleagues who have helped me become whole over the years—to all of you I am eternally grateful. I also would like to thank my friend, Lisa Bielawa for helping me make my words coherent. And to Alan X.—I appreciate your honesty and hope that this rare illumination into pedophilia from our conversations will help protect children in the future, a goal which I know we share.

# Introduction

What motivates child molesters? What drives them to seduce and violate children again and again, sometimes over many years? The little that we know has not been learned from the perpetrators themselves, (Pryor, 1996) thus giving us an incomplete picture.

There is much in this book that is shocking, frightening—even sickening. But if knowledge is power, we can learn how to protect our children and, perhaps most importantly, teach them to protect themselves.

Empowering our children so that they may protect themselves is a critical mission of this work. While many books have tried to address the issue of abuse prevention, they have not sought solutions that empower children to protect themselves from sexual abuse. Too often, professional advice concerns itself with recognizing symptoms of abuse that is already happening or offers only vague rhetoric about improving communication.

As strange as this may sound, it's important to realize that though children are the victims in any child sex abuse case, often they are consenting victims. They keep the sexual abuse secret, and they accept whatever dubious "rewards" the abuser may offer. People worry that in teaching children about certain dangers their innocence may be compromised or destroyed.

This need not be the case. We need to empower children, to strengthen their sense of identity and personality so that anything the potential molester might have to offer will have no appeal. The tools and strategies included here will help instill in a child a sense of self that is unassailable. And this, I believe, is the real key to preventing abuse.

Alan X., as I shall call him, is a convicted child molester. He was arrested in the late 1980s after sexually abusing children for decades and was charged with hundreds of sexual assaults on minors. He remains anonymous so as not to cause further pain and distress to his family or his victims.

None of the proceeds from this book's publication will reach him. Rather, a percentage of the royalties will be donated to the International Society for the Prevention of Child Abuse and Neglect.

Before he went to prison (near the age of fifty), Alan was also the man next door—a Boy Scout leader, a deacon in his church. He was, by all accounts, an upstanding member of his community.

He also abused more than one thousand little boys.

The powerful first-person account of Alan's criminal history and his offenses against children is included in these pages. It may shock you. It is jarring and upsetting to read. In writing about his own pedophilia, Alan gives us an extraordinary gift. He has shed light on the most shameful criminal secret.

For the sake of simplicity, I refer to child molesters, sexual offenders and perpetrators as "pedophiles" and "he." That is not to say all who sexually abuse others are male, which is certainly not the case, but that the use of "s/he" is visually jarring and detracts from the potency of the message within this book. And because most children are sexually abused by active pedophiles, I will utilize that term primarily.

The conversations reported in this book came from both face-to-face contact in music therapy sessions, sporadic telephone calls over the years, and written interchanges in letters spanning an entire decade. Often I would pose a question in my letter and Alan's written response would answer it as if we were actually speaking to one another.

I have combed through thousands of pages of his writing and condensed them into autobiographical segments within the chapters. His writing is eloquent, intelligent, and insightful. In fact, at times, Alan's writing style seems more like that of a doctor than mine. The reader may find this disconcerting on many levels. One of them may be that we wish to believe that child molesters are not as smart as we. Yet that often is simply untrue.

Alan's purpose in writing is to let people know how they can protect their children. With complete honesty he describes his actions and subsequent guilt. He asks for no sympathy from the reader and makes no excuses. He simply illuminates the twisted workings of a pedophile's mind.

Because Alan will spend the rest of his life in prison, he has nothing to lose by telling the truth. He wants only to open our eyes. If we are willing to see what he shows us, we—and our children—have everything to gain. We can finally understand more fully how and why the pedophile lures and molests his victims, and gains control over their minds and bodies.

Alan tells exactly what it's like to be a monster. We learn how he selects his victims, what qualities he looks for in a child, how he decides which child is vulnerable to sexual abuse and which child he should avoid. He describes for us what extraordinary lengths the molester will go to in order to avoid detection and tells how proposed legislation might actually serve to escalate the level of violence inflicted on our children by child molesters.

We learn from Alan that pedophilia is an orientation forged in childhood. He began sexually abusing younger children when he himself was a young child. He is now in his sixties. Were he not in prison, Alan would still be abusing children.

As a music therapist, I use music as a therapeutic tool to aid in understanding and communicating with people. I first met Alan when I was working on a maximum-security forensic unit, helping to evaluate prisoners for mental illness prior to their trials and/or sentencing. I had been a music therapist for a decade when I met Alan. I had worked with several populations, but primarily with those having psychiatric illnesses. One of the men on the unit, Alan, had refused to speak with all other professionals—psychiatrists, psychologists, social workers, guards, and nurses. When I introduced myself to Alan as the music therapist, he responded by saying, "If you want to understand me, listen to my music." The staff was shocked. Until that point he had been unresponsive to intervention of any kind. Alan had shut down completely. He hardly ever left his cell, rarely made eye contact, and showed little interest in anything. It was only because I approached him with the language of music, a language he considered his own, that he allowed me to enter his strange world.

I was qualified to work with Alan for another reason,

though he didn't know it for many years into our relationship. I had been a victim of childhood sexual abuse at the hands of known and trusted primary relatives. From the age of four years until shortly before my grandfather's death when I was nine, I suffered regular, unthinkable sexual assaults by him and by my father.

I kept the secret of their crimes against me from everyone, and for years, even from myself. I examine in depth the process by which those repressed memories were awakened as part of my own contribution to this book. Even repressed, my history as an abuse victim did much to forge my identity, my choice of career path, and my professional interests. As a therapist, I had always been able to relate to the victims of sexual abuse. Until I first recovered memory of my own abuse, (at age twenty-six) however, I hadn't realized why.

Although I had worked for years both with child abusers and victims of sexual abuse, it wasn't until I worked with Alan that I began to understand my own history. I learned how the pedophile systematically strips a child of self-respect, trust, and, finally, the ability to say no. I learned why I kept my terrible secret, and why I felt the need to protect my abusers. I was forced to look at the way I'd been manipulated by men who used their authority over me in the most heinous way imaginable. I learned why, as a child, I never had a chance to avoid being a victim.

Processing this life-altering knowledge was painful. My sessions with Alan were so intense and emotionally charged that there were times when I considered resigning as his therapist. After sessions with any other prisoner, I would immediately record my clinical observations in my personal log. With Alan, I would need to wash my hands (physically and metaphorically) after our meetings and have a meal alone.

I had to nourish myself with food in the aftermath of those wrenching encounters before I could analyze my clinical and personal observations. Being with Alan brought me face to face with many of my own demons, and more than once, I wanted to turn and run away.

A doctoral advisor, Dr. Margot Ely, researcher and author of *Circles Within Circles*, once told me "all research is me-search." In my case, this has certainly proven to be true. As much therapy as I had undergone to understand the ramifications of having been abused—as much therapy as I had given others—it was Alan's exceptional intelligence and insight that enabled me to finally understand the mind-set of the abuser and the abused. This empowered me to put many of the ghosts of my past to rest.

The book you hold in your hands has been ten years in the making. It has taken that much time to sort through the thousands of pages of Alan's writings to isolate the pertinent passages. It has taken a great deal of time to formulate an analysis of Alan, since his insight into himself, his behavior, and his understanding of his crimes has evolved so dramatically over the years. It has taken ten years for me to reach the point where I am able to face my own experiences.

These pages offer hope and healing to those who have survived the ordeal of childhood sexual abuse. By sharing this story of a truly incredible relationship, I hope that I can inspire others and help to free them from their pasts. Sometimes the most therapeutic discovery of all is the sheer knowledge that you're not alone, that what happened to you has happened to another. If I can heal myself, I believe there is hope for everyone.

When I began this book I had no idea that I could be happily married, blessed with children, and living a life that had seemed like an unattainable dream. I had felt doomed to a life of independence, too scared and scarred to open my heart to a partner. I have been personally fulfilled through this work and hope to give others a vision of the attainable. Most of all, it is my greatest wish that this book's publication will serve to help protect the futures of children everywhere.

This book constitutes two extremely personal journeys—Alan's and mine. By weaving our stories together, Alan and I hope to place valuable tools and information in the hands of concerned parents, educators, legislators, children, and the public at large.

The sexual abuse of our children is the ultimate, and perhaps final, taboo of our society. Whereas alcoholism used to be a very private, behind-closed-doors "problem," today even the catchy phrases of organizations to help alcoholics are used by everyone. We see alcoholism as an illness, a disease. While cancer used to be a term often uttered aloud only in a hospital setting and frequently kept hidden from even those who were being destroyed by it, today it is an acknowledged "public enemy" and treatments are discussed openly. Even AIDS, with its associated sexual and drug related overtones, is entering the forefront of our nation's consciousness and billboards are displayed in most public places.

In sheer numbers, pedophilia ravages more lives than any of the above. Why then is it not getting the attention it demands? We must quickly answer this question and hasten our attack on this devastating epidemic.

## CHAPTER ONE

*Amy:*

# The Beginnings

I first met the man I call Alan in the late 1980s. Since then, I've been over that meeting in my mind a thousand times trying to imagine how I might describe it to someone else—wondering what there was about that particular afternoon, this particular prisoner, that was so very different.

At the time, I was working as a music therapist in a maximum-security unit. In my years of specialized training and experience in my practice, I have seen extensive evidence that music can serve as a powerful form of communication and self-expression when conventional therapies fail. The lyrics of a particular ballad, the strains of a half-forgotten lullaby, the steady rhythm of a hand-held drum—all of these can provide a critical means of accessing and expressing feelings where ordinary conversation cannot.

That was certainly true in my first encounter with Alan. Perhaps we were somehow drawn to each other because he seemed as out of place as I did among the brash, arrogant younger prisoners and the indifferent, cynical guards and staff.

To the rest of the unit, we must have seemed an unusual pair. Thin, rather frail, Alan was considerably older than the other men. His wire-rimmed glasses and graying hair made him look more like a college professor than a criminal. The withdrawn, downward cast of his eyes and mouth betrayed a severe state of depression, even despair. I was even more of an anomaly on the unit—in my late twenties, but petite in a way that made me look younger, with long blond hair cascading down my back. And I always carried the tools of my trade—a set of hand drums and a guitar.

In those days, even getting onto the forensic unit was something of a challenge. I was an attractive female entering a maximum-security, all-male facility. Many of the guards made no attempt to conceal their hostile feelings toward me. The instruments I used and I myself were subject to searches. I needed to walk a fine line, because in prison, it's the guards who make the rules. Too much familiarity was dangerous for me; being aloof, on the other hand, could get me in even bigger trouble.

Each of the prisoners in this particular unit was being evaluated for mental illness prior to his hearing. Alan was no exception. I could see him following me with his eyes as I made my way slowly through the day room, introducing myself as the music therapist. I came to the corner where Alan sat alone, isolated from the guffaws and crude jokes of the rest of the men. I stood by his side and he never took his eyes from the guitar.

"If you want to understand me, listen to my music," Alan said in a voice so soft that it was little more than a whisper.

The staff attendant nearby shot me a startled glance, and I was confused by his reaction. I took another long look at the man who sat in front of me, clasping and unclasping his hands as he stared at the instruments. What I didn't know was that Alan had refused to converse with any other professionals until that afternoon. In fact, although he had already been on the unit for some time, it wasn't until I stood in front of him, guitar in hand, that Alan spoke spontaneously to anyone at all.

It was a dramatic moment because everyone else in the unit had written him off. Alan was completely shut down. He hardly ever left his cell and showed little interest in anything. But we spoke the same language—music. And, as I was to find out, music is a language without lies.

I chose a small side room, away from the clamor and hubbub of the rest of the floor. For those who have never visited a prison, it's difficult to imagine the constant level of noise. The low murmur of hundreds of voices form a background roar, punctuated frequently by the shouts of violent arguments that burst out of nowhere. The echoes of the cell block, the rattle of food and supply carts, the rhythms of the guards' constant patrols—the result is a strange and deafening symphony from every quarter, twenty-four hours a day.

We had our first and every subsequent session locked in that side room, with a guard standing outside the Plexiglas window in the main area of the unit. On this and every forensic unit I had worked on, I was always ultraconscious of where my back was, where the door was located, and what sounds were around me. In this particular room I sat in the corner and kept my back to the wall, facing out toward the unit window. Alan, too, had his back to a wall and his profile to the window, watching over his shoulder. I sensed that whatever he had done, he was more afraid than I was.

I began with a few soft chords on my guitar, asking Alan about his favorite songs. Something flickered in his eyes as he thought about it. When he spoke, his voice trembled with emotion.

"Do you know "House of the Rising Sun" [by Alan Price]?"

I did and began to play. As I reached the first chorus, Alan joined in, his whispery tenor gaining strength as we sang:

*Oh mother, tell your children*
*Not to do what I have done*
*To sell your soul for a pocket of gold ...*

I listened intently to the lyrics Alan chose to sing. Thoughts flashed through my mind as I analyzed his selections. What was he telling me through this song? What had he done that sold his soul? How would children follow his lead?

The song was originally about a gambler returning to New Orleans to serve a jail sentence. Obviously Alan was in jail, but I was sure the resonance of this song for him went beyond the similarity of circumstances. The song was a sad, somber one that contained no hope, no redemption, only a warning to others not to do what he had done.

I did not know why Alan was on the forensic unit for I had made it my practice to first see the prisoner before reading his chart in order to have an opportunity to form my personal opinions without knowledge of his past. But something began to emerge in that first session, hints of what he might have done. Many of the almost two dozen songs we played in that first session revolved around the themes of childhood, loss of innocence, and terrible and sinister manipulations. "Puff the Magic Dragon" (by Peter, Paul, and Mary) mourns the loss of childhood. Crosby, Stills, and Nash's "Teach Your Children" and Billy Joel's "Billy the Kid" were others among

Alan's favorites. He was telling me about himself through the music; he was trying to reveal what he had done. They were songs of isolation and estrangement, songs of loss, and always, *always*, songs about children.

While singing "Billy the Kid," Alan showed emotion for the first time when he reached the words, "he didn't have a family, and he didn't have a home." He looked like he was about to cry. The lyrics to "Teach Your Children" also seemed significant to him. He nodded in agreement while singing, "You, who are all alone ... teach your children well ... keep them on your side." Luckily, I knew each of his selections and genuinely liked them. We shared a common musical dialect.

Alan's musical choices and songs struck a chord of empathy in my own heart. Every therapist is also a human being, and though I could surmise already from that first session that Alan had done awful things, I did not and could not see him as a monster. His musicality revealed him to me as a fellow person.

When I read his chart after our first session, I was not surprised to discover that Alan's crimes were against children, for a part of me had already known the truth. The music had opened the window onto his personality, and in the coming months, would reach him the way no other medium had or could have.

We met once a week for more than a year. Though most of the men on the unit came and went, Alan remained, partially because it was dangerous for him to be placed among the general prison population and partially because, after the initial charges of child sex abuse were brought against him, other victims came forward. Alan's case snowballed, and a long and appalling history emerged. He had victimized approximately one thousand children. Week by week, month by month, I had to struggle with my own horror as more and more of the terrible truth was revealed. Of course I was shocked and angered by the sheer number of victims he had molested. Research shows the average pedophile abuses approximately 250 children (United Youth Security, 1999).

Little by little, Alan recalled his crimes and described them to me in detail. His confessions disgusted me. Yet I had to sit, listen, and even respond as he told his tales of torturing children. In our early sessions, he described his crimes as a kind of game with rules of his own invention. Psychologically, his pedophilia compelled him to act out a fantasy world in which he controlled everything: the thoughts, impulses, bodies, almost the souls of his victims. It took months of sessions before he was able to make any emotional connections at all. He was eventually able to recognize his blocked feelings, and after still more time, to show them by his expression and voice.

Little by little, through what I call a musical free association, Alan began to open up to me. I would play the melodies of his favorite songs, and he would recite whatever lyrics came to mind. These lyrics were potent puzzle pieces. We returned to one of his favorites, "Puff the Magic Dragon." Though its precise meaning has been hotly debated for decades (many feel the song alludes to drug use) certain passages were uncannily relevant to Alan's history. He had told me that only boys between the ages of six and thirteen were appealing to him, that after puberty they no longer held the attraction for him. Alan recalled the poignant lyrics, musings that little boys grow up, but dragons remain ageless. This song served as an opening for Alan to describe the otherwise indescribable.

His favorite songs functioned not only as a communicative vehicle in our music therapy sessions but also in a similar fashion on a much less intense scale during his previous life before prison. For example, when Alan was feeling conflicted, he would play "Love on the Rocks" by Neil Diamond on the jukebox at a small local bar. The bartender once commented to Alan, "She must have broken your heart," probably thinking that a painful breakup with a woman was Alan's reason for selecting this song. By nodding in agreement, Alan was able to make contact with another adult about his internal pain while not revealing anything about himself. We discussed these lyrics from the song:

*First they say they want you,*
*Then how they really need you,*
*Suddenly you're out there ...*

Through the discussion that arose from these lyrics, I came to understand how pedophiles manipulate their victims into engaging in chronic sex abuse. Alan described the manipulation of his victims. First he would get the boy to want his attention and then make him feel that he actually needed Alan in his life. For better or worse, I was allowed into Alan's experience.

The music helped me connect with Alan on an emotional level. The melodies and harmonies allowed the words to flow between us. Since I already had an affinity for much of his music, it was possible to regard him in a less negative way than I might have otherwise. The songs offered us a safety net. Although our work was emotionally taxing for me, the positive experience of sharing this music gave me strength to persevere in my quest to understand more fully the horrible nature of child sexual abuse.

Week by week, I struggled to see past the sickness and into the person, to stay in touch with whatever feelings of empathy I could muster. But something specific helped me in this struggle, kept me coming back. Alan was not at all like the father and grandfather who had abused me nor were his crimes anything like those I endured, but emotionally I knew I had come face to face with the monster. If I could stay with him, learn about him, and help him understand the damage he had done to his victims—if I could get Alan to *feel his feelings,* he could *somehow make his life worth something.* And if I could do that, I might finally conquer my own past.

# CHAPTER TWO

*Amy:*

# Treating the "Monster"

The insights I gained during my months of treating Alan continue to flourish within me years later. I found myself understanding my own sexual abuse in a much more profound way. Even though there were differences between my sexual abuse that was incestuous and the pedophilic sexual abuse inflicted by Alan, the similarities were striking. And although I had always known intellectually that I was not able to stop the abuse from happening, that as a child I couldn't have had the requisite knowledge or understanding to do so, I came to realize how little control I actually had in my situation. My vulnerability went way beyond a lack of knowledge.

I understood how powerful my abusers were and how powerless I was. I looked back and reviewed instances of abuse that seemed on the surface to have stemmed from my own initiative and was finally able to recognize the web that had actually been woven insidiously by my abusers. My past was now making more and more sense to me, which in turn made my life in the present more potent. The music I listened to and played, as always, was my lifeline. I especially sought solace by composing my own music during the period I was treating Alan.

Music also had a powerful emotional component for Alan. His usual reserve would slip away as we improvised on the drums or guitar. He would cry or shout in anger about the horrible things he had done to children. Little by little, we unlocked his feelings of sadness, anger, and unbearable guilt, and eventually he was able to recognize and admit to the extreme damage he'd inflicted.

Once the flood of his emotion was released, his remorse was so great that he wanted only to die.

Between sessions, Alan wrote extensive notes and gave them to me to read and keep. Because I was only with his unit on Thursdays. I knew nothing of his mental or physical status from week to week until I saw him with my own eyes each time.

He tried to commit suicide a number of times by such bizarre means as swallowing a toothbrush and bits of floor tile. Even a prisoner on a maximum-security unit can find a way to end his life. The uglier the crime, the less likely the guards will protect the prisoner from himself. Some of the guards made Alan's suicide attempts relatively easy, if only by virtue of looking the other way at a critical moment. Other guards took a more active role, by attacking him at night or by making his crimes known to particularly violent inmates. Because of his age, Alan was unable to defend himself against stronger, younger, and more violent men. In the year that we worked together, he was threatened, attacked, and urinated on. I never knew if I would find him alive.

And each week I had to face all over again my own con-flicting feelings about the value of a life like Alan's. Wouldn't it be better for society if he were dead? Wouldn't it be better for him to kill himself, instead of living in constant danger, waiting for death at the hands of cruel guards or violent inmates? Could even a life like Alan's have any purpose? Was trying to unlock his secrets and his emotions the cruelest punishment of all? Still I never walked away.

Although I've had therapeutic experiences with many other incarcerated pedophiles before and since, none had ever revealed his inner feelings with such insight. I had the privelege of seeing Alan's world through his eyes.

Alan's writings reveal a man of considerable intelligence and awareness. We all like to believe that anyone capable of committing such crimes must be a monster. However, I learned that when the monster is revealed, he is never anything more or less than a human being.

This realization was difficult for me to accept. All I would ask is that you don't allow your initial shock and revulsion to turn you away from the truth of what he and I have to say. Alan allowed me to understand why abuse occurs in the first place. This understanding is the key to prevention.

My contact with Alan has certainly been an extraordinary journey. And I hope this sharing of our innermost thoughts and feelings will accomplish our purpose—to sensitize people to an issue that has for too long been a terrible secret.

# CHAPTER THREE

*Amy:*
# Feeling Different

Although Alan and I seemed as different as two people could be—he was old, I was young; he was incarcerated, I was free; he was the mental patient, I was the therapist—we were on common ground about sexual abuse. The thread that ties victims and perpetrators together, probably the single most prevalent characteristic among pedophiles and their victims, is a distinct feeling of being different from everyone else.

On the surface, the implications of a sense of difference might not seem very significant. Just about everybody believes that she or he is somehow different. Each of us has individual talents, preferences, idiosyncrasies, abilities, and handicaps that set us apart. For the stable, healthy person, a feeling of uniqueness generally reflects a healthy state of self. For the pedophile, this sense of being different is neither healthy nor realistic, but rather a justification for seeing himself as separate from society and a "victim" of fate.

It is a mental means of disassociating from mainstream society and an attempt to avoid all levels of personal responsibility. For the victim, feeling different means feeling painfully cut off from others on a profound level. A kind of permanent loneliness keeps the victim from connecting with others and enjoying life fully.

Before his child victims evolve emotionally, long before they assume full control of their own minds and bodies, the abuser intervenes and thwarts the process. These children are unaware that many other children who are also victims have experiences like theirs and share the feelings of differentness. They feel isolated. And as we all remember, nothing is as important as feeling part of a group to children and adolescents.

Sexually abused children know, of course, that other children eat, sleep, and go to school as they do, but that's where the similarity often ends. As youngsters, we learn quickly that our peers scorn or mock anyone who appears unique, and we try our hardest to fit in. As young children, we instinctively learn not to broach the subject of our sexual knowledge, which we have acquired because adults are sexually familiar with our bodies. We know our peer groups think that sexual acts are "nasty" and those involved in them are "bad people." We learn fast to keep our sex lives secret.

As abused children, we feel that our bodies are different from those of our peers. In addition to the already disorienting physical changes that all young bodies undergo, we have experiences and reactions that are uncommon. Our bodies are prematurely sexualized. Prepubescent boys may have erections that their peers do not, and prepubescent girls may experience orgasms due to their early sexualization.

These bodily functions are scary and disconcerting, and worse, they alienate these children's bodies from their owners. They make their owners feel damaged, as if their bodies no longer belong to them. And indeed, in a sense, they don't. They are physically child bodies that have been treated as adult bodies.

Feelings of being different go much deeper than the physical realm. A child is no longer truly a child once he or she has been victimized sexually. Typical children's games often seem meaningless to the child victim, and his or her sense of joy disappears. This child is unable to let go of inhibitions in a spontaneous, childlike way after his or her body has received adult treatment. This child may play out scenes over and over with toys and objects but will derive no pleasure from them.

By the age of eight, I hardly understood why my peers played games. They seemed useless to me, but I knew I should try to join in so that I would appear "normal." My idea of recreation was to hide up in a tall tree for hours at a time with a book and a supply of food, or to hide in large bushes that I called "forts," decorating them as one would a home. One was even furnished with a used Christmas tree!

I loved to dress up in disguises, wigs and long skirts, and wander around my neighborhood hoping that nobody would recognize me. It's not surprising, given my ongoing sexual abuse, that in the summer I would beg my mother to allow me to ride my bicycle in the neighborhood without a shirt on. I would wear a baseball hat over my short, cropped hair and delight when shop owners referred to me as "son." I felt much safer when no one could see me as the vulnerable girl I was.

When I wasn't hiding out in some way, I was busying myself in self-destructive ways or in what my mother termed "minisuicides." I would jump from roofs of houses onto nearby bushes (forts) or sit outside my house on the corner along a busy street and then dash out into oncoming traffic. Even when joining in a school game of softball, I stepped from the catcher position directly into the swing of the bat, allowing it to smack and injure my hip. Sometimes I decorated my toes and eyes with my mother's makeup, attempting to make them look bruised and battered in order to get attention. This kind of confused activity replaced play for me. At other times, I would try to hide actual serious injuries I sustained through various accidents when I should have received attention for them.

Looking back, it seems to me that I swung between crying out for help and almost giving up on life altogether. I felt so different from others, so dirty and bad, that it seemed impossible even to try to relate my experiences to anyone. I had no words for these experiences anyway.

Music provided a source of connection, even if only to invisible or fictional "others," for me in my sense of isolation as a young child. I played guitar and piano and listened intently to popular songs. There was one song in particular that reached me, "Shilo" by Neil Diamond. The words, which I still hear vividly in my mind to this day, describe a young, lonely girl feeling that the only friend she could find was in her mind.

I felt the singer was singing about me. A song can serve not only as a vehicle for self-reflection but also as a way to address the unspeakable, particularly for a child. The music expressed the mood and the lyrics helped label or describe the specific events that created the feelings. I came to understand the feelings of different-ness that are universal among victims of childhood sexual abuse through memories from my own childhood as well as through subsequent music therapy work with patients.

In my clinical experience as a music therapist, I remember Sue, a girl who, I'm sure, felt different from other children. She was a shy and nervous eight-year-old, a newcomer to the already-existing music therapy group who had come to the hospital with a diagnosis of depression. On the unit, she was generally polite and superficial and made little contact with her peers or the staff.

During one of her first music therapy groups, she listened to another group member, Dana, talk about her favorite song, Suzanne Vega's "Luka." This song portrays a young girl who is abused in her home but tells the neighbors not to ask her what is wrong. After the song ended, Sue spoke very quietly to Dana. "That's like my house." Dana knew what Sue was talking about and replied, "It's mine, too." Together they began to sing the lyrics and speak about the similarities between their lives and the life of the girl depicted in the song.

The group, which was usually loud and rambunctious, sat attentively as the girls spoke. I played and sang the song on the piano, leaving spaces for them to fill in their own names and experiences. Soon the entire group was singing this personalized song together. When the session ended, many of the members offered Sue signs of support—kind words and hugs. During her hospitalization, she was especially friendly with Dana. Sue continued to open up and speak about abuse in her home during our sessions. For her, speaking about her abuse not only helped to alleviate her feelings of drastic different-ness, but also enabled caregivers at the hospital to acquire the information they needed to intervene in her home. Music can alleviate our feelings of aloneness if we can let ourselves hear it in a therapeutic way.

As with much else in my life, I considered music to be serious business. It became a true therapy for me. I didn't listen to it for mere enjoyment with others, only intently and in private. I didn't just play guitar for fun; I signed a contract when I was ten years old to help teach guitar classes. Music was certainly a lifeboat for me, but when I was a child, it was a lifeboat with a one-person capacity. Although I felt different from others, I was always outwardly seen as a very social creature, gregarious, cheerful, and full of energy. I participated in many activities with my friends and listened to their tales of woe but remained as neutral or silent in regard to my personal life as I could, and my relationship with music remained intensely private.

When I was twelve, my girlfriend and I were riding our bikes to the record store (to buy my first record!), and a car ran into me in the parking lot. I was thrown off my bike and was lying on the ground when the driver and his passenger got out. Both men were holding beer cans. They screamed and cursed at me for getting in their way, then they roared off.

Shocked store owners, customers, and my friend ran to my assistance and wanted to call my parents or an ambulance, but I didn't want to draw attention to myself. I felt that somehow I was responsible. My friend and I picked up the pieces of my bike, and I hobbled home. She tried to reassure me that I had done nothing wrong, that I was riding in a safe manner, but I was convinced that if the men told me I was in the wrong, I must have been in the wrong. I knew that my friend wouldn't have hesitated to call her parents to the scene if she had been injured, but I felt that my situation was "different."

I hid the pieces of my bike in a bush behind my house. I tried to walk upstairs to my room to lie down, but I couldn't lift my leg high enough to reach even the first step, so I knew I had to tell my mother I was hurt. I received medical attention for my broken tailbone, but I was too ashamed to give my parents the slip of paper a witness had thoughtfully provided with the license of the car. I felt that I deserved what had happened to me and that only I was to blame. I was left feeling vulnerable and alone, and I suspected that I unconsciously broadcast my fragility to everyone in my sphere, no matter how hard I tried to appear strong and confident.

When I was thirteen, as I was walking on the sidewalk, I was approached by a young man of perhaps eighteen or so on his bike. He rode toward me and leered at me in a way that made me feel nervous. I clutched my books to my chest. As he passed, he slapped my buttocks. I kept walking, feeling fearful and shameful. I felt sure that, even though I had purposely dressed in baggy, androgynous clothes, he sensed that my body was "different" from other children's bodies, a body that invited hurt. I felt that it was the sexualization of my body that provoked his behavior, and I felt ashamed.

He swung his bike back around, and I could see that he had his hand on his exposed penis, protruding from his unzipped jeans. He calmly told me that he was going to rape me. I had only one option for escape, which was into the enclosed porch of a house directly behind me. I bolted to the door, praying that it would be unlocked. It was. Imagine the surprise of the family eating dinner as I flew into their house, madly locking their door behind me. As I shakily explained my actions, the father leaped up and went looking for the bicyclist, who had fled. I called my brother to come to walk me the rest of the way home.

I don't remember if I told my mother about this encounter, but I do know that the police were never notified. I remember telling my best friend's father about the occurrence. His first question was "What were you wearing?" which caused me to feel even more shame about what had happened.

Approaching puberty, I realized that my friends' homes

were drastically different than mine. They confidently walked right in their own front doors with me; I had to peek in first to ascertain my father's stage of drunkenness. Their fathers laughed and joked with them. They did things as a family, like going to restaurants or taking vacations.

I remember my feelings of emptiness when I accompanied a girlfriend home once after a clothes-shopping expedition. She had purchased a gorgeous outfit costing an exorbitant $72, using a credit card that her parents had loaned her. Her father looked at the outfit and said how lovely she would look in it. He told her that she should have bought more like it! Then I returned home with my meager purchase of a blouse for less than $10. Although I tried to sneak in quietly, my father blocked the way and insisted on seeing my purchase. He berated me for spending so much money on something as senseless as clothes. Even though I had used my own babysitting earnings for my shopping, his response left me feeling unworthy of spending my own money on myself.

I watched with envy as my friends' fathers attended their sports events or drove them to activities. I felt that I had such a different life from theirs, even though I lived in the same neighborhood and went to the same school. Above all, I felt that it was my fault that my life was so different, and that if I were a better person, my father would interact with me the way my friends' fathers interacted with them. As a child, I felt as many other victims feel—different.

Sexually abused children find it almost impossible to communicate to others about their experiences. They feel that they are to blame for what has happened to them and that they will be punished. Feelings of self-disgust run so strong that the child is certain that any possible listener will share these same feelings of repulsion for him or her. This fear locks away the possibility of communicating feelings to disclose crucial information to those who could help. For these and many other reasons, reaching out simply does not happen, and the child is self-defeated.

What is so distressing to me is that although both the victims and offenders with whom I've worked experience feelings of being "different," the victims feel ashamed and blame themselves for their different-ness, while the offenders feel they are different by chance, by default, or by circumstances out of their realm of responsibility.

# CHAPTER FOUR

# *Introducing Alan*

Alan's analysis of his own feelings of "being different" took place over years of correspondence with me. The passages below are excerpted from letters spanning many years. In his descriptions of his feelings, one can sense both important similarities and important contrasts between the aloneness of victims and the aloneness of offenders.

*Alan:*

I was the youngest of three children born into a middle-class working family. My parents tried to provide everything that they thought their growing family needed. In many ways I was a fortunate youngster for I never really wanted for any physical necessity nor was I ever subjected to any form of physical abuse.

While my physical needs were well attended to, my family itself operated in a very cold, detached, and formal fashion. Ours was a house filled with reasonably bright people, but communications between us were more an exercise in intelligence and civility than a genuine sharing of feelings, experience, and concern. At a very early age, we learned that each person was responsible for handling his own problems, and we really seemed to be more of a collection of individuals, all of whom were wrapped up in their own efforts at surviving, than a family unit.

The entire family circled around a single hub, my father. There was never any question as to his being the head of the house, and his personality, likes, dislikes, fears, prejudices, and insecurities formed the center core of our existence. My parents were hard-working folks who, for reasons of their own, seemed either incapable or unwilling to show any feelings toward anyone but each other. Together, they appeared to have formed one joint personality, and they never risked letting anyone else get too close to them. They were good people, but they were obsessed with keeping the world at a distance.

Very early in my life, I recall them being involved in social activities outside the house, but as time progressed, they steadily withdrew from just about everything and everyone. Eventually, there were very few visitors to our home, and it was not the type of environment that you wanted to bring friends into. Looking back, it seems to me that my parents were Victorians, and out of place in a changing world. They believed that if you could keep life polite and strictly formal, you could deal with it without becoming emotionally involved.

At the age of six or seven, which is the earliest I have realistic memories of, I was a confused, frightened little kid. Nothing around me made sense, and no one around me seemed willing to provide much in the way of explanation. In this cold, uncommunicative, and impersonal environment, it seemed to me that I was the only one who couldn't understand things.

I was forever doing something that violated some unwritten family code. In my house you were expected to know the answers and were taught, early on, that if you didn't, it was your job to find them. When I did screw up on a reasonably regular basis, the reaction I encountered was amazement at my being so inept, usually followed by some statement to the effect that "you really ought to have known better!"

One of the early lessons my father taught was that "successful" people never show their emotions. I can distinctly remember being repeatedly instructed, "If you allow other people to see your emotions, you have given them a weapon to use against you." In my father's world, it was all right to feel something, but totally wrong and dangerous to allow that feeling to be seen by anyone else. It appears, in retrospect, that my father was attempting to take a behavior that worked for him in the business world and incorporate it into a lifestyle for his family.

Demonstrations of affection were nonexistent, and I cannot truly recall either my siblings or myself ever having been hugged or kissed by either parent. As I reflect about this period of my life, my overwhelming feelings are of being in a constantly cold, unfeeling void, surrounded by strangers who apparently wanted to remain as such. I was in a setting where I felt stupid and out of place; I felt "different" from the people around me.

When I entered school, life became even more confusing. These new people, my classmates and teachers, were nothing like the people at home. This was a world of noise, emotion, and direct confrontation, all of which were beyond my experience. At home, nothing was dealt with in a direct manner. We all scurried around the fringes of things in a conscious effort not to get "involved" in "other people's affairs."

At school, the rules were totally different. I spent these early years in a spinning limbo. If I behaved at school the way I had been trained at home, I didn't fit in; and if I attempted to behave the way the people at school did when I got home, I very quickly got put into my place.

None of this made sense to me, and the only thing that I realized was that I didn't seem to fit in anywhere. 1 spent the rest of my school years drifting back and forth between these two totally different environments, feeling like a misfit in both.

It wasn't long after I started school that I discovered masturbation. Although I viewed everyone around me as being different from myself, I enjoyed sharing this pleasure with another kid. Shortly thereafter, I began my first crude attempts at acting out. I was about seven or eight at the time, and I was almost immediately caught engaging in sexual play with a boy a couple of years younger than myself. My mother's emotional reaction to this incident (something I will describe in greater detail when I discuss the role of secrecy) had a tremendous impact on me. She was horrified.

For the only time in my life, I witnessed her being emotional and out of control. She dragged me into the bathroom and attempted to "scrub" the dirt off me, while screaming, "only twisted, sick, and evil people do things like that!" (I should point out that the "offense" in question amounted to mutual fondling.) Her major concern, and something that she kept hysterically repeating, was to keep my father from finding out that I was "sick."

At this point, she decided to punish me in a rather strange way. She gave me a punishment but insisted that we tell my father it was for doing something else. She pointed out that if I were to divulge the real reason for my punishment, the consequences would be much, much greater. From the moment that I left that bathroom, the relationship between the two of us, my mother and me, became totally adversarial. She was now my enemy, a person who shared a part of a dark secret and who constantly watched me for other signs of my being "different."

As I lay in bed that night, masturbating and fantasizing as 1 always did, I realized something that had not been a part of my thinking before that day. I reasoned that if only sick, evil people enjoyed masturbation, and I obviously loved it, then I really was a sick, evil being. In my childish mind, the logic seemed perfect; the reason why I didn't fit in with other people was that I wasn't like them ... I was different.

I break here to add what I feel is an important observation. If anyone jumps to the conclusion that what I have outlined thus far "made" me into a pedophile, he or she would be wrong. What I have attempted to describe might show the beginnings of my feeling "different" from others, an aspect of my developing personality that I would later use as a justification for my actions, but this series of circumstances could easily have been encountered by another individual and not resulted in his becoming an offender.

I believe that there were a multitude of factors that led to my choosing to act out, and that those which I have mentioned here are only to show how early in life I saw myself as being "unique."

# CHAPTER FIVE

# *Alan:*

# My Parents

My parents did everything they thought was right in bringing up their children. Although I might wish that they had done certain things differently, I'm convinced that they always acted in what they believed to be the best interest of their family.

To be honest, this is not a view of my parents that I have always held. For a very long time, I disliked them intensely and hated what I felt "they had done to me." Looking back, however, I realize that this type of focusing was just a way I had to keep myself in the victim role.

While people and circumstances have played a role in my development, it was me who pulled the pieces together in a way that served what I thought was in my personal best interest. Even at this early stage of my life, I was a very scared person. I didn't like dealing with other people because I didn't understand them and was always afraid of being rejected or hurt.

Prior to my being caught acting out, I felt different but couldn't understand why I felt that way. Now, I had a way of justifying all of my failures, shortcoming, fears, and frustrations, a perfect Catch-22. I didn't act like "them," after all ... "I was different." In my childish way, I had begun not just to build my identity around my sense of difference but also to see myself as being a victim.

Instead of facing the reality of my situation, I turned the object of my desire into something that I claimed to detest. The mental gap between "my" world and "their" world grew larger and larger with each passing year, as did the amount of time that I spent fantasizing and acting out. My growing sense of difference became my total sense of identity. I used my self-created sense of victimization as a tool to justify my thoughts or actions.

I saw myself as a person who, "through no fault of his own," was deprived of a "normal" life. And as I convinced myself that I had been somehow cheated by fate, I felt I had a license to do anything I chose to. If I didn't play by their rules, why should I? I was never allowed to "play in their game." If I wanted to force some smaller child into having sex, why shouldn't I? After all, I was the real victim here, not him. This self-created and self-serving sense of victimization allowed me to do anything that I desired without the slightest twinge of guilt, shame, responsibility, or remorse.

By my early teens, I knew I was a coward. I was constantly terrified of my peers and elders, but here again, my sense of "difference" allowed me to explain away my shortcomings. All I had to do was remind myself that it was quite natural for a person to be afraid of people who were different from him, and thus reminded, I felt fully justified in both my fears and my actions. Although I felt vulnerable and incapable in the world surrounding me, I could always offset those feelings by acting out. I could, at any time, make myself feel stronger and more in control of life by forcing some even more vulnerable child into submitting to my will.

This single aspect of life seemed to be the only domain that was within my control and the only activity that provided me with any sense of pleasure, power, and, in a twisted fashion, acceptance. Sexual fantasy and sexual abuse became my total panacea. I sexualized everything in life and took out all of my pent-up feelings and frustrations in sexual and sexually aggressive ways against more vulnerable victims.

It was during this period of my development that I feel I began to identify totally with my sickness. I didn't see myself as a person whose sexual drives and desires differed from those around me but as a totally and irrevocably different being from the rest. I didn't see sex as a part of life but rather as the sole purpose of my existence. And, as my focus centered more and more around my sexual difference, the mental gap I felt between myself and all other people grew wider and wider. During my teen years and thereafter, I felt nothing in common with anyone else. Regardless of whom I might be with, I felt alone, defensive, and different. Every activity, every relationship, and even every conversation was affected by my sense of difference and my increasing obsession with keeping that hidden difference a secret.

Of course, this point of view was a total distortion of reality, a total self-created, self-serving set of defenses and justifications driven by my fears. But for a terrified, cowardly, and paranoid youngster, it all seemed very, very real. And, because I viewed it as a reality, it became one for me. I clung to the feeling of being different because I was too scared to face the reality that I wasn't. I built an entire alternate reality for myself so that I could avoid having to take responsibility for my own insecurities, fears, and character defects.

What made any understanding of the importance of my communication shutdown difficult for me was the fact that it was such an incredibly subtle process. While severing effective relations with the rest of the world may have been occasioned by some strong emotional trauma, it happened at such an early age and with such totality that I have always viewed it as "natural," just a part of my being "different" from the rest of the world. I withdrew before I really understood that I was withdrawing and then "grew up" accepting that alienated state as my "norm."

To my mind, there is no single more destructive feeling in childhood than the icy horror of feeling isolated, inadequate, and totally alone. In that mute, alienated state you feel totally trapped, hopelessly vulnerable, and both frightened and angry. When a child has lost the ability to trust and communicate, he has lost his only means of getting the nurturing needed to counterbalance the fears and distortions in his small world.

All of us encounter a wide variety of adverse situations and influences in our lives, but most of us are fortunate enough to trust someone at least to the degree that we are willing to "risk" communicating our fears, feelings, and confusions. The delicate but essential lifeline of interpersonal communications allows us a means of straightening out the mess in our minds, facing our fears, and continuing to grow. The simple, or seemingly simple, act of dealing directly and as an equal with the world around us gives us a crucially needed element in our developing and maintaining a stable, healthy, positive sense of personal identity.

# CHAPTER SIX

## *Amy:*
# Childhood Sexual Dysfunction

Alan is a homosexual pedophile; I was a girl incestuously abused by men. And yet, the sexual issues were the same. In our years of correspondence we never discussed the topic of sexuality in isolation, because in the structure of sexual abuse, sexuality is only part of a composite total. Although our respective stories of sexual abuse depicted very different players, we shared a specifically sexual sickness that was like a shroud covering each of our lives, starting from a very young age.

Instead of doing what most children do—experimenting with things, questioning everything, learning to deal with feelings and fears, and eventually moving on to discover new challenges and interests in life—future pedophiles withdraw as children into a fantasy world, armed with a self-created sense of being "different."

While many children participate in exploratory sexual play in early childhood, they typically don't become obsessed with it. It seems that the healthy child can experience this phase and having satisfied his or her curiosity, quickly move on and become immersed in the process of discovering the world. Pedophiles reach this point and stall developmentally. Sexual stimulation becomes the focus of reality, and all of life becomes one gigantic sexual experience.

Even the most neutral incidents can have sexual overtones for victims. This heightened sensitivity to sexual nuance begins when they are children and continues as they grow. A simple pat on the back from a friendly teacher can be misinterpreted as a request for a sexual experience. The child will interpret any favoritism from someone with a sense of foreboding, assuming that sexual demands will result.

Alan's revelations about himself brought insights to the surface of my own consciousness. I recalled that as a child I was frightened and isolated, and that I could not respond to overtures of friendship or approval without suspicion.

Since these mis-interpretations are carried into adult life, it's no wonder that victims' subsequent relationships are often seriously impaired. The victim experiences life without discerning which stories, words, or gestures have sexual overtones. They often read sexuality into nonsexual stimuli or remain oblivious to the presence of sexual intent when it is evident to others. This confusion about sexual signals also contributes to one of the darkest aspects of sexual abuse. Once abused, a child is more likely to attract the attention of other sexual abusers. The pedophile knows how to identify the behaviors associated with a child's patterns of misunderstanding.

For example, when I was in high school, I had a girlfriend whose father was a band director from a neighboring junior high school. He occasionally conducted our band as well. Although she and I were not very close friends, he slipped into my life as a "pal" because of my relationship with her.

Looking back, I think Mr. M. must have sensed that I was a vulnerable target. Carefully and slowly, he began to intrude into my life by showing his vulnerability and neediness. He learned that I had completed my lifesaving and water safety instructor certifications, so he began by calling me at home and repeatedly asking me to teach him how to swim. I naively believed that this was what he truly wanted.

There was nothing secret about our relationship, and no one warned me that it was strange for a teacher to have such a strong interest in a student his own child's age. I began to meet him once a week at the YMCA to give him lessons. Our lessons involved some physical contact at first, since they dealt primarily with his breathing, and then none as they progressed. Later, my leg was in a cast, so I had to teach him while standing on the deck of the pool.

Mr. M. seemed unhappy that I could no longer be in the water next to him, but I was certain that my injury did not compromise my teaching, and reassured him that I could call out instructions from the poolside. I was flattered that he chose me to teach him how to swim, but I began to think it was a bit odd that he would also call me up to ask my advice on his conducting style with our band. I finally attributed his behavior to his separation from his daughter, who was with his estranged wife, from whom he was in the process of getting a divorce.

After my leg healed, he offered to reciprocate by teaching me how to play golf. I accepted, thinking that it would be fun, and he picked me up one afternoon for my first lesson. It was also my last. As we approached the first tee, he stood behind me, pressed his erect penis against my buttocks, and wrapped his arms tightly around me, allegedly to show me how to hold the golf club. The sudden imposition of him forcing his body onto mine in such an obviously sexual way shook me up enough to react immediately. I began to cry and demanded to be taken home. I was so repulsed by him that I rode the entire way back with my head out the car window, trying to stay as far away as possible from him.

At one point, my baseball hat blew off, and as he slowed to stop to retrieve it, I insisted he continue driving. I didn't want to spend one more minute than I absolutely had to with him. I was so shocked that he had a sexual interest in me, yet how could I not have seen it before? Swim lessons and phone calls?

Just as my early memories were blocked off, and perhaps because of it, my own sexuality was also blocked off for many years. In high school, when most teenagers are actively dealing with the awakening of their sexuality, it was inconceivable to me that anyone would be interested in me for my body. I knew I was popular and was reasonably attractive, with a slender figure, yet I thought that boys' interest in me was purely for my wit or brains or friendship. Time after time, when I would be alone with a male "friend," I would be stunned when hands began to roam my body.

I didn't want this kind of attention—it did not feel good—but I remained silent. Somehow it was ingrained into me that if someone desired me, then I must comply. So I did, holding my breath, hoping it would end soon. It was not an option to decline, to voice my objection, or even to be unavailable the next time a boy came to visit.

As a teen, I was lucky enough to have some long-term boyfriends who were truly interested in my whole package, and I found those relationships fulfilling, both physically and emotionally. But the casual friends whose sexual advances I could neither desire nor deter were horribly burdensome.

The only limit I managed to set with them was that they were not to remove my clothes. I felt that as long as the fondling only happened over or under my clothes I remained a Catholic virgin. This stipulation was very important to me, and somehow I was able to verbalize it to them. I felt that it was my duty to keep them happy by allowing them to fondle me in bushes or pools or in small rehearsal studios. I was powerless because I could not understand two basic realities: Through their actions they were expressing interest in my body; and if I didn't desire them physically in turn, it was my right to decline. I had no perspective on the situation because these simple concepts were not part of my emotional vocabulary.

Victims often display a lack of understanding of this kind of fundamental. The younger a child is when he or she is sexually abused, the more difficult it is to help him or her understand even the basic reality of the abuse, let alone heal from it. Their perspective is already impaired. Many child victims with whom I've worked can only see in another person what is protruding from their body.

Child victims of recent or ongoing molestation may masturbate excessively, grope at other's crotches, stare at female breasts, and punctuate their speech with sexually flavored comments. Regardless of how their bodies appear, they feel that their genitalia are practically visible to any observer and that they are always exposed and vulnerable, as if they are naked.

These children's drawings often include exaggerated sexual organs and distorted body parts. When they play with dolls, their games contain elements of traumatic play, such as dressing and redressing dolls over and over without deriving any joy from it. Such play is called traumatic because it is an attempt to rework an upsetting situation, and there is no pleasure in it as we would hope. Their games with action figures explode with violent destruction accompanied by loud sexual expletives. Even mealtimes provide stimuli for sexual innuendo, inspiring comments about the size or texture of the food. And these examples are taken only from the observable, accessible areas of these children's lives.

Many arenas of my nonsexual life are distorted even today as a direct result of being forced to have oral sex. The sound of food being chewed or sucked loudly causes me to have visceral feelings of repulsion, disgust, and rage. Whether the sound emerges from a radio, telephone, or in my immediate environment, I cannot control the feelings that well up inside.

I realize it's only the sound of eating and not the sounds that accompanied my own sexual abuse. And I can intellectualize that my overwhelming feelings are inappropriate for the current situation. But I cannot control my visceral reactions and often have great difficulty modulating my responses. At best, I can hide my feelings of repulsion, disgust, and rage, and frequently I can remove myself from the upsetting sounds. But at times I still snap nastily at the innocuous offender, demanding that the eating stop immediately.

Another involuntary response I have from my own sexual victimization is that I cannot tolerate holding an object between my lips for more than a couple of seconds without gagging violently. It's amazing, especially when caring for my two young children, how many times a day two hands are not enough. I often need to put a pen, piece of paper, bib, or toy between my teeth for a few moments so that my hands can help a child.

Despite my knowing on a very real level what the object is and why I need to hold it in my mouth, my body still responds in a visceral, involuntary way, thereby sexualizing a simple, daily, and very nonsexual aspect of my life. The sexualization of daily life seems to have no gradations for victims of sexual abuse, only black or white. This proves true for perpetrators as well.

# CHAPTER SEVEN

## *Alan:*

# My Childhood

Whenever I've told people that I started acting out sexually before reaching my ninth birthday, and that by seven or earlier, I was masturbating on a nightly basis, they seem totally amazed. They can't understand how I managed to become sexually active at such a tender age. I think that part of their amazement is based on a misunderstanding of what was actually happening at that time. They're looking at this form of early sexual stimulation in adult terms, whereas what was taking place was something that does not fit into the adult definition of sexual gratification.

My initial attempts at masturbation were purely physical acts that resulted in my feeling physical pleasure. To the best of my recollection, when I began doing this, my actions were not brought about, or accompanied by, any type of sexual thoughts or fantasies. At the age of seven, for example, I did not lie in bed at night picturing a child whom I found physically attractive and then gratify myself by means of masturbation. Initially, my fantasies were totally nonsexual; and initially, my "playing with myself" was solely a separate physical act.

Webster defines "fixation" as "A strong, often unhealthy attachment or preoccupation." I've often tried to figure out at what age I reached this point of being fixated, but about the best I can come up with is at the point when I joined my use of fantasies as a means of escape with my use of sexual stimulation as a source of physical pleasure. I am convinced that I did this very early in my life and that beyond that point nothing else really seemed either important or interesting to me. Most people would think my sexualization of life began with my having been sexually abused, but that simply wasn't the case with me.

It might sound strange to most people, but I began creating my own distorted little world at such an early age that I can't really recall ever having the slightest feeling that I would, could, or wanted to live a "normal" life. When I was ten or eleven, I can clearly recall that people would say things such as, "Just wait until you're grown and have children of your own." I would calmly but without any hesitation reply that this was never going to be. The adults who made those comments laughed at what they thought was my youthful naiveté, never for a second suspecting that the child standing in front of them had already closed the door on most of what they thought of as "normality."

In my self-created world, where I saw myself as isolated, inadequate, scared, and victimized, I had discovered what I thought was an escape, and once I discovered it, I focused all of my time, attention, energy, and intellect into pursuing it. Once I made the link between my fantasies and my developing sexual drive, I began to see the world in an entirely different light. I started to view everything around me in terms of its possible sexual application and potential.

In essence, I began to sexualize my entire life.

Because all of us have different interests in life, we see things in the world around us primarily as they support our interests. Each of us, seeing the exact same physical object, sees it differently, relating it to our own special interests.

I suspect that the amount of time we spend trying to invent applications for a given object is directly related to the degree of potential we see for it within our area of interest and the degree of potential obsession we have for that particular interest. A stable person would probably see an object that held potential for one of his interests, grasp the idea, file it away for later use, and then quickly move on to other things. A more obsessed individual, one with fewer interests in life, is more likely to spend a great deal more time attempting to make that object fit into his limited world. For me, it was an all-or-nothing mentality.

Either I could see or invent a use for an object within my single-faceted world, or I viewed it as being totally worthless. For example, when I was around twelve or thirteen, at Christmas, I received an electric train set. As soon as I unwrapped the present and saw what it was, I focused on how it could be set up in the basement as a means of luring neighbor boys into spending time down there with me. The trains were nice, but I only truly appreciated receiving them when I saw a potential for their being used to feed my perversion.

By judging objects in this fashion, I was filtering out any parts of life that I didn't see as serving a sexual purpose. I was actively working to support my view of life as a totally sexual experience. Unfortunately, inanimate objects were not the only "things" that I began to judge in this manner.

As time went on, I began to apply the same type of sexually-based judgment to the activities in which I chose to be involved. Little by little, I was closing out the real world, drawing a tight, totally sexual circle around myself. I was ridding myself of anything that didn't fit in with life the way I wanted to see it.

At fourteen, I decided to join the Boy Scouts. Obviously, for a young teenager there was a wide variety of school, church, and social activities opening up for me, but this one held a special interest. Most boys who enter scouting do so at ten or eleven, an age when I had absolutely no interest in being involved in any activity that forced me to associate with peers, older boys, and adults. At fourteen, however, I had what I saw as an age advantage, and while some of the younger boys were more advanced in scouting than I was, my being a teenager automatically provided me with status and an element of control.

By joining scouting at fourteen, I made what I believe was my first conscious decision to participate in an activity solely for the potential victims that it offered me. I didn't suddenly drop all other involvement and begin to exclusively "hunt" younger children, but it was a definite escalation in my sexualization process.

At fourteen, I was at an age when continuing to associate with boys who were significantly younger than myself was bound to draw undue attention and unwanted suspicion. Now that I was entering high school, my immediate access to a school-supplied pool of potential victims was gone, and the age gap between my victims and me was noticeably wider.

I needed to find safe ways of being around ten- and eleven-year-olds. Like many scout troops, the one at our small church wasn't getting much adult support, and the scoutmaster was delighted to have a teenage volunteer to help with the younger boys. It was this experience that taught me the usefulness of being useful. I learned that as long as I was providing some type of service for the adults, they didn't seem to question my being there.

This playing a useful role as a front for offending was not lost on me, and it became a tactic that I regularly employed for the rest of my life. Deciding to enter scouting was the first step in a process that continued to escalate until, as an adult, I'd only involve myself in an activity if I saw a real potential for it being sexually rewarding.

During this period, I was careful to continue participating in those activities that helped me maintain my "typical American teenage" image, but these involvements were seldom something that I looked forward to or felt satisfaction from. I viewed them as necessary evils. It was also during this midteenage period that I began the final stage of my conversion of life into an exclusively sexual state. My conscious judgment of people was based only on their value in providing fuel for my perversion. For several years, I had been doing this with young boys—seeing them strictly as sexual entities—but in my midteens, I expanded this concept to everyone. I started looking at the adults around me in light of their either having a son(s) in the age group I wanted or having some connection with an activity that involved boys that age.

One example of my early use of adults as a means of gaining access to victims comes immediately to mind. As a teenager, I wanted to molest the ten-year-old boy living next door. The problem was that he was too young for me to pal around with without causing suspicion. I needed some way to get to spend a reasonable amount of time with him but to do it in such a manner that no one thought anything about it. Although these people lived in the very next house, my family did not get involved with neighbors. I started watching them, trying to figure out some innocent way of establishing contact. After a while the answer became apparent: Be useful! The husband was frequently away on business trips for days at a time, and in his absence, I often saw his wife struggling with manual chores around the house and yard. I decided that the next time I had an opportunity to help when she was having problems, I'd grab it.

Before long the husband was off on business, and she was in the backyard trying to start a lawn mower that refused to cooperate. I asked if I could help, and without waiting for an answer, took over the task. I started the flooded mower and wheeled it back to the garden shed for her. She was delighted and offered me a tip, but I just smiled and said, "It's nothing." Having accomplished my goal, I took off. What I wanted was for her to tell her husband how helpful the boy next door had been, and for him, when he next saw me, to come over and at least say thanks.

The way I figured it, if he was coming up to me, and I knew about his coming ahead of time, I would have an advantage in directing the conversation; I would be in control. And, if for some reason he didn't do as I expected him to, I would continue being helpful in small doses until he almost had to make contact. I would lay in bed at night fantasizing about the impending meeting. I developed various schemes designed to get me alone with the child, and I kept attempting to arrive at an approach in which I could find no flaw. For several nights, I pictured every aspect of this encounter, refining details, and even taking it to the degree of designing a workable script.

I'd like to point out that while I ended each of the nightly fantasy/planning episodes by masturbating while picturing myself involving the child in sexual acts, the majority of the fantasy had nothing to do with the boy. It was totally devoted to developing the initial approach.

Once I felt I had the plan to the point where it would probably work, all I could do was wait for the father to take the first step.

A week or so later, when I was in the backyard cutting weeds by the fence, the husband came over, thanked me for being so considerate to his wife, and offered me a tip. I again turned this down, saying that it really wasn't a big deal, just a couple of minutes work letting the mower drain and then putting it away. Then I used the set-up line, which I had so carefully rehearsed. "Besides, about the only thing I ever charge for is baby-sitting."

He seemed surprised that I did baby-sitting, and I quickly pointed out that I only looked after older kids, like the ones I worked with at church and in scouting. Having planted the seed, I excused myself and headed back to the house.

I knew that he often took his wife out on weekends, particularly when he had been away during the week. I also had seen a variety of local girls used as sitters. My bet was that he would prefer using a boy, particularly one who worked at church and in scouting, and that it would be much simpler for him to have a baby-sitter who lived next door. Now the only thing I could do was to wait and see if this seed of an idea would take root.

It did. While I was waiting to see if they would call me to take over as their baby-sitter, I continued my nightly fantasies, but now I concentrated solely on the child and worked to develop a plan for getting him into a position where he would do exactly what I wanted.

I relate this because it shows how even in my early teens I was seeing and using adults as pawns to provide me with victims. By fourteen, I had figured out that manipulation, planning, and patience were much more effective than rushing ahead and taking unnecessary chances. And, by once again serving a useful purpose, I was able to create a situation in which my spending long periods of time with the boy was his parent's idea. In essence, the parents were now delivering the child to me as a means of accommodating their own needs, freeing me from further suspicion.

The purpose of these examples—the train set, the scouts, and the neighbor—is to give some insight into how I was steadily transforming all of life into a sexual exercise. As with most types of escalation, I didn't suddenly leap into each of these three stages to an obsessive degree but rather edged into them bit by bit. Not every planned strategy worked out according to my fantasy, but enough of them did to leave me with a heightened desire to continue using this approach.

I point out again that not every pedophile has the same experiences that I have had or carries things to the same degree. My life is one from which I hope you can gain some small insight into the general workings of a pedophile's thought pattern. While the individual experiences vary, I believe that the fundamental concepts, the factors that go into making up the distorted mental world of a pedophile, are very similar in most cases.

Sexualization is a closing-off process. By focusing virtually all of my attention on feeding my perversion, I created a self-feeding distortion of reality. However we do this, we begin to see all of life in purely, or predominately, sexual terms. And to support this vision that we want desperately to see, we block off every aspect of life which we cannot make fit our perverted aims. Not every pedophile goes to the same lengths in sexualizing life as I have, but all of us seem to engage in a major degree of sexualization.

## Chapter Eight

*Amy:*

# Warning Signs

Modern-day preteens in general are more absorbed with their budding sexuality than previous generations of preteens, which is evident in the way they dress. Even their style of dancing is much more seductive than ever before. The window of time during which our children can be considered presexual is shrinking each year. What we see on a daily basis in the media reflects our interest as a society in sexuality.

It is a rare television show or commercial that appears without targeting this interest. As a music therapist, it's amazing to observe the evolution of sexual material in our popular songs. I remember somewhat sexually suggestive music in the mid-seventies, such as "Popsicle Toes" by Michael Frank, which uses geographical terms with undeniably sexual connotations: "I like to feel your warm Brazil and touch your Panama."

Back then I was not surprised that many radio stations banned this song. Compare this example to the explicit illustrations of sexual acts found in much of today's hits. How does this intense overstimulation affect children who may already be too preoccupied with sexuality? I'm speaking not only of children who were abused but also of the hidden population—young people who are beginning to victimize other children sexually.

Parents of budding predators are generally unaware of their children's sexual interest. Society's taboo against discussing abuse and one's own private denial and fear of childhood sexual abuse make it almost impossible for parents to consider the possibility that their child may be a novice molester. Does your child seem to isolate him or herself from peers? Is she or he preoccupied with Internet sites? Does she or he seem to spend inordinate amounts of time in inward reflection? Are there amounts of time and/or money missing that are unaccounted for? Does she or he show a strong preference for spending time with younger children?

Parents find not only comfort but also even pride in having a child who seems more interested in younger children than peers. "Jessica is the most sought-after baby-sitter in the neighborhood. She's so loving to all the children." "Jason puts his athletic skills to such good use by coaching soccer every weekend for hours at a time as a volunteer!" "We never have to beg Sue to watch her cousins; she even does it for free." "Frank is so mature—he takes the little boys under his wing, lets them help with his paper route, and even takes them out for ice cream."

What's wrong with these pictures? How cynical must we be? Can we not allow for goodness to flow forth from our children without immediately judging it in a perverse way? The old adage holds true: Better safe than sorry. It does no harm to investigate, quietly and sensitively, circumstances that seem out of the ordinary when children are involved.

Even parents who are already slightly suspicious tend to allay their concerns by rationalizing and intellectualizing. "It's no wonder Joan always runs out of her allowance the next day—she's too generous with the young kids next door," or "Tom is gone every afternoon and never seems to be able to recall what he did, but the poor boy feels so shy about his weight that he is probably trying to exercise or diet and just doesn't want us to know."

Of course we want to think and believe the best about our children, and the thought of them engaging in an activity that is genuinely morally reprehensible is intolerable to us. But why treat sexual abuse differently than a physical illness? Wouldn't we, as parents, investigate a physical concern we have about our child's welfare? When a child shows signs of being oversexualized, we must remember that the child's very essence—his or her emotional and sexual being—is ailing and urgently needs our intervention.

There are, of course, parents who have been confronted with actual allegations that their children have sexually molested other children. Usually an allegation involves only one child; everything is so rapidly hushed thereafter that rarely is an inquiry broadcast to see if there are other victims. These parents are often aghast and quickly find refuge in the belief that the sexual incident was "only sexual exploration" and will never happen again. Perhaps they seek individual therapy for the child, which often serves to isolate him or her even more.

Groups for youths who are accused of sexual misconduct are not widely publicized. Meaning that most young perpetrators suffer the fallout of the discovery of their behavior utterly alone. This contributes to their feeling even more isolated and different from other children than they did before. In private therapy sessions, the child usually minimizes the discovered incident and may remain silent about dozens of undiscovered molestations. Eventually these children are released from therapy, having learned only how to be much more secretive and careful.

Schools and health professionals often have children in their care for a limited time. Therefore, each discovered incident may be the only one that comes to light in its particular context or environment. Single allegations may be more readily dismissed than they would be if the child's entire history were made known.

At a facility where I was a therapeutic consultant, I was dismayed to see the way the administration responded to an incident involving three patients. These boys resided in a residential treatment center for children with emotional problems. The older boy had long been interested in younger boys. He often tried to hug and play with them, and the staff was wary of his interest. They tried to keep his hands off of the other children. Imagine the anger, betrayal, and sorrow of the victims' parents when they learned of the inevitable incident. One night he slipped past the aide and molested two young roommates, one a recent arrival, in their beds. These were disturbed children with psychiatric problems who had been sent to this facility to receive help and be kept safe.

When the families were told about the molestation, the parents with money hired attorneys, and their young child was moved to another branch of the institution. The other family had few financial and political resources, so they were forced to accept that their child would remain in the same cottage with the perpetrator. The staff could not send the molester to a facility for young offenders since this was the first actual allegation against him that was confirmed. He remained in the cottage with many other children, all of them at risk.

Although it is clear that these parents should have had access to some way of protecting their children, I do not believe that simply locking up a young offender will solve the problem. Without treatment focusing on his or her sexualization of life, there is no safety or security for either the offender or the younger children around him or her. An added danger is the explosive emotion of parents of victims.

I remember a fight that broke out between two grown men, probably parents at a children's hockey game. One of them, angry that the other allowed unnecessary roughness, beat the other into a fatal coma in front of the children. The tragic irrationality of this act demonstrates that the response of parents to those who jeopardize or violate their children's safety can be just as violent as the acts that inspired the rage. Picture this hockey parent as a father learning of his child being sexually abused by the next-door neighbor. Violence to the offender and his family is a strong possibility when the incidents are discovered.

No one is safe as long as we ignore signs of inappropriate sexualization. Just as with alcoholism, knowledge about the nature of sexual abuse has evolved over the past few decades, and yet we *must* become more open and aware of the pervasiveness of child sexual abuse in our culture. We must not discount any possible avenues of access to child victims. Molesters find and use any and all such avenues avidly. Our children continue to be at great risk.

# CHAPTER NINE

*Amy:*

# Fantasy

The definition of fantasy in the dictionary is "a creation of a creative imagination." The act of fantasizing is a normal diversion for most of us, something to help depressurize difficult situations and flavor an often-bland routine. While the act of fantasizing might, in and of itself, be a totally innocent respite for the stable mind, it can very quickly become a dangerous and destructive tool for those whose mental state is one of addiction and/or perversion. Fantasy plays an important role in the life of every pedophile. Many describe their bouts of fantasy as "sudden" and "overwhelming." These fantasies play an essential role in their sexual acting out, and this chapter begins to illustrate how this happens.

Fantasy is also an essential element in the lives of victims of pedophiles. Since their experiences cannot be shared, they must use their own psychological methods to escape the pain of abuse. These methods can range from wishing for a magical savior to dissociation, repression, and even the development of multiple personalities. (The phenomenon of the occurrence of multiple personalities as a result of sexual abuse appears often in psychological trade literature, notably in the book *Guilty by Reason of Insanity* [Lewis, 1998].) These methods are still in place long after the sexual abuse ends; they impair even adult survivors' judgment.

In my own case, my distorted thinking contributed to my making a poor judgment in my choice of my first husband. I had the fantasy that things were not really as they seemed and would get better, despite warnings from my friends and colleagues that my choice was clearly based not in reality but in wistfulness.

My husband was a wonderfully gentle, caring, and patient man who was ten years my senior, a college professor who was a foot taller than I, and almost twice my weight. I was a student in his department at the university when we began to see each other secretly. My close friends joked that he filled the role of a father figure for me. I agreed and thought that I may well need some fatherly love since I hadn't experienced much of it growing up. I had always had a blank in my memory that erased everything prior to the age of thirteen. I couldn't remember things like what schools I attended, or the houses in which I had lived.

In my teens I thought that people who claimed they remembered their elementary teachers must be lying. I thought that no one could remember childhood things that vividly. Eventually, in college, I began to think that perhaps I had blanked out these memories because of the *emotional* abuse I incurred while living with an alcoholic father who had never wanted any children and ended up with five of them. He certainly made it clear that he did not enjoy our presence in his life.

When I married for the first time at the age of twenty-two, I tried to believe that, although our sexual intercourse was extremely painful to me, that aspect of our relationship really wasn't so important. I rationalized that because we got along fabulously as platonic friends, we would be able to hold our marriage together. The pain associated with sex was puzzling to me because our premarital sex had been painless. It wasn't until our honeymoon that the unbearable pain began.

Immediately upon our return from our almost uncon-summated nuptial holiday, I sought medical attention. Several appointments and exploratory gynecological surgeries later, no physical problem had been detected. Then, four years into our marriage, I had an affair at a music therapy conference, which was my first extremely pleasurable sexual experience. As I returned home from the conference, I wept through the entire four-hour flight, as memories began to flood my mind. I vividly recalled houses I had lived in, complete with rooms in which I had been molested. I was astounded that I could sud-denly remember so much. I was horrified that memory after memory of my father and grandfather sexually abusing me burned vividly in my mind. Over and over I recalled in detail elements of one of the scenes of my sexual abuse in which I was lying on my back on my grandfather's bed. My father was kneeling at my left side, holding down my stomach and throat, while my grandfather pushed his erection into my mouth. I suddenly comprehended why I had always had cer-tain neuroses, like my violent aversion to seatbelts pressing down on my stomach or sweaters touching my throat. These were the parts of my body that had been held down in order for the abuse to take place.

I returned home to my life as a graduate student and wife, but I immediately visited the library and began to read every book I could find about sexual abuse so I could understand why I could suddenly remember my earlier childhood. As awful as it was, I was relieved to have access, finally, to my own biography. I finally had memories of my first thirteen years. I learned that the device I used to prevent severe emotional damage from my sexual abuse was called repression. Encouraged, I believed that I could go to a therapist, which would be the first time in my life I had done so, get over the fact that I had once been sexually abused, and then be able to continue living happily with my husband. I fantasized that our lives would remain unaltered.

One month after my memories returned, I had the first dream I had ever remembered in my twenty-six years. In this dream, my mother hit me over the head with an object, and as I called out "Dad" to have him come to my rescue, my husband came instead. I awoke with a jolt, realizing that the two men were one and the same as far as my body was concerned. For the first time, although I knew I had married a man who was clearly a father figure to me, I discovered that my husband and father even looked alike. I had never allowed myself to notice the resemblance. It was no wonder my body responded to my husband so differently before and after our wedding. Sex with my husband felt incestuous to me, and my body held that memory, even when my mind hid it from me.

These initial beliefs were replaced by others. I rationalized that we could simply reformat our relationship. Meanwhile, I could not even lie in bed chatting with my husband without my arms wrapped tightly and protectively around my stomach. I didn't feel safe enough to rest them behind my head. All the while he had always been loving, kind, and tender with me.

I thought we could live apart for a while, see each other each month, visit each other's therapist, and learn to desire each other sexually. It was only after years of trying to put sexual interest into our relationship that we finally gave up. I realized that it's one thing to rekindle a sexual energy that has dwindled, but it's another thing entirely to attempt to spark sexual chemistry that had never been ignited in our marriage. It took many years after my husband gave up and asked for a divorce before I could let go of the fantasy that we would be reunited much later in life, perhaps after retirement, when sex was no longer so important! Fantasy certainly ran a large portion of my life.

Child victims' purposeful use of fantasy begins almost immediately after abuse starts. They wish for imaginary beings to fly down and rescue them. Among my reclaimed memories is that throughout my childhood, I wished and dreamt nightly that I would sprout wings to help me fly away from my abuse. My fantasies never included the desire for my attackers to be killed, only for the abuse to end. It is difficult for children to be responsible for punishing a loved one in fantasy, and they often create fantasies that involve win/win situations or magical interventions, like a mysterious gravity that floats the offender away from the victim. When we teach our children that sexual predators are "bad and evil" and must be punished, we add weight to their troubled feelings about loved ones who may even seem simultaneously loving and hurtful. This kind of moralizing makes disclosing the abuse even more difficult because children know that if they "tell on" their attacker, he will be sent off and hurt.

Fantasies that remove oneself from the situation simply by disappearing don't give rise to these conflicts. If we were to teach our youth that pedophilia is a sickness, we could introduce the idea of disclosing abuse so that the predator can get help (while still being kept away from committing other sexual offenses). This possibility allows the child to exist in a much more tenable situation. She or he no longer has to fear naming the bad guy, rather the child could know that his abuser would be getting help for his sickness.

This approach does not excuse the pedophile for his actions but is meant to treat the sickness and better safeguard others. I heard Maya Angelou speak (May 14, 2001, Purchase, New York) about her childhood sexual abuse. Immediately after her rape, Angelou named her rapist, and he was incarcerated for one day. Shortly after he was released, his corpse was discovered. He had been kicked to death. Upon learning of his fate, the nine-year-old Angelou became mute for many months. She believed that because of her words, this man was killed. She didn't want to risk doing such damage with her words again. What if the response had been different when she spoke up? What if she had been given help to recover from her rape while her perpetrator received proper treatment and surveillance, instead of the nightmare that actually ensued? Most sexual abusers prey on children who they know well. What we as adults fantasize as just punishment for sexual molesters may differ dramatically from what the victims themselves wish for.

For victims of sexual abuse, fantasy often follows their abuse, whereas for pedophiles it usually appears before they act. Both believe that their fantasies control their lives.

For much of Alan's incarcerated life he has been in a special sexual offenders' unit. This has enabled him to have lengthy conversations with many other pedophiles and he has learned that in many ways his experience is not entirely unique. Even though aspects of sexual abuse such as "fantasy" may seem idiosyncratic, many core elements can be generalized from one pedophile to another.

# CHAPTER TEN

## *Alan:*
# My Disturbing Fantasy World

Most of the pedophiles with whom I've talked want to see their imaginings as being totally involuntary, something over which they exercise no control. I always chose to think of my fantasies in that fashion and clung desperately to this same self-serving concept. This distorted way of looking at my fantasies allowed me to continue fantasizing for as long as I pleased and let me carry my imaginings to any height of perversion, while still seeing myself as an unwilling participant in the process.

Had I admitted that my fantasies were totally a product of my own creation, I would have been forced to face the ugly truth, that I was doing exactly what I wanted to, and enjoying it tremendously. In order for me to continue enjoying the "thrills" and sense of escape my fantasies provided without having to accept responsibility, I had to view them as I chose to view everything else in life, as something outside of my control, something I was "forced to endure."

For many of us pedophiles, fantasies and/or masturbation are old, old habits. They have become our panacea for dealing with every situation, feeling, and emotion that we don't want to face. For a lot of us, fantasy has provided a mental escape since early childhood, and the habit of creating a private world of delusion is so deeply ingrained that we want to believe it's something that we can't actively control. We make the choice to create these fantasies, but we have been making the same choice for so many years that we have virtually assured ourselves that it is an automatic reflex and not a conscious decision. In my personal experience, I can attest to the fact that fantasy is a fertile feeding ground for escalation (upping the ante in order to achieve sexual satisfaction). Using my own life as illustration, let me attempt to show you how my use of, and dependency on, fantasy grew in direct proportion to my fears and insecurities.

As I have pointed out, pedophiles want to see themselves as victims in order to justify their not setting any personal limits. Seeing ourselves as the ones being victimized allows us to do anything without any real sense of guilt or responsibility. For anyone who wants to perpetuate a view of himself as a victim, fantasy is a very effective tool. Even in creating our fantasies, however, pedophiles attempt to find ways of avoiding responsibility.

It was not until I actually attempted to put this story on paper that I realized that my fantasies could be divided into two distinct types. One type is sexual or sexually sadistic in nature, while the other, the oldest type, is totally devoid of any sexual content. I used both of these mental escapes at different times in my life, and I feel that it's worth touching on them separately. Again, I ask you to keep in mind that these represent my own creations, and I am not suggesting that all

pedophiles have precisely the same fantasies or escalate following the same time schedule.

The oldest type of fantasy that I can recall, and one that
stayed with me up until quite recently, was never sexually ori-
ented. In these imaginings, I would picture myself as an
orphan, and on many occasions a boy suffering from some
form of physical handicap or from some type of nonsexual
abuse. These fantasies centered around a rather typical "Little
Orphan Annie" plot line, i.e., unwanted and unloved child
suddenly finds love and acceptance in the adult world. In
these imaginings, I always saw myself as a child whose difficulties were never products of his own doing, and it's interesting to note that these fantasies never contained any other
children. Over a period of forty years, I did very little to alter
the basic plot.

I don't recall what age I was when I first began to create
this type of fantasy, but I do know that it was close to the age
at which I began school, perhaps six or seven. I find in looking back that even at this early age, I was inventing scenarios
in which I pictured myself as a victim. This means of escap-
ing a real world that I didn't want to face quickly became a ritualistic part of my daily life. I should point out that these fantasies didn't just pop into my mind. They were things that I
intentionally created and always created at bedtime. I won't
attempt to interpret the themes [of the fantasies], except to
say that they clearly seem to cry out of a desperate need for
acceptance. I used this type of mental pacifier every night
until I developed a sexual variety, and even after I began developing sexual fantasies, I would, on occasion, revert to these
earlier conceptions.

Not too long after I created this first type of fantasy, I
discovered masturbation and began to alter radically the cen-

tral theme of my nightly fantasies. It seems logical that I was doing this during my early school years and close to the age at which I began acting out sexually; sometime around seven or eight. Similar to my early fantasies, this new breed was restricted to my bedroom, immediately prior to going to sleep each night. Long before I was physically capable of achieving ejaculation, I still found tremendous satisfaction in this act and made it a fixed part of my nightly routine.

In the early stages of this second type of fantasy, my imaginings were kept at the level of picturing a younger boy, whom I found myself attracted to, and coercing him into performing what I viewed as "mutual" fondling and masturbation. Over time I escalated the type of activities that I fantasized about, moving from masturbation to manipulating the victim into performing oral sex. In every case, the child whom I fantasized about was an imaginary being, not someone I knew in real life. The imagined victim (although I did not see the child as a victim at that point of my life) had to be thin, very bright, and usually physically small for his age. I wasn't overly concerned with such details as hair color or facial features, but each victim had to be both thin and younger than myself. I was a heavy child, and my imagined victims needed to represent everything that I felt I wasn't.

These fantasies were extremely general in nature. I would not spend a lot of time creating detailed, involved plots. The fantasies were usually brief and ended as soon as I could achieve a climax. During this period, many of my fantasies dealt with finding what I viewed as a "perfectly willing, although initially shy" victim. While I changed the background settings and physical appearance of the victim from time to time, the overall plot remained one of fundamental willingness with just a bit of manipulation on my part. I soon found myself expanding these fantasies, attempting to increase the overall thrill.

This new series of fantasies seemed to break from the previous pattern, where I had seen myself as the victim. Now, although I tended to try to make the acts imagined mutual, it was clear that I had transformed my role from victim to victimizer and that I was increasingly enjoying the feeling of power.

Somewhere around nine or ten, I began to fantasize about kids whom I actually knew. Lying in bed at night, I would run through a mental list of classmates and neighbors and select one to serve as the object of fantasy for the evening. In doing this, I was not content with just placing a known child into an imaginary setting. Now that I had an actual target in mind, I found it more exciting for me. I don't think that I initially saw these more highly developed plots as the beginnings of my conscious planning for actual molestations, but it wasn't long before I began to suspect that if I could make someone my victim in fantasies, I might be able to use the developed pattern to make that same situation a reality. Here again, the fantasies had escalated.

The connection between fantasizing and using fantasizing as a means of developing plans for later implementation was still pretty much in an embryonic state at this point. While I might spend more time working out details, I was still hesitant to try creating the same situation in real life. I was, however, finding this new form of fantasy more and more exciting, and I was making these nightly rituals longer and longer. During this period, I still treated each night as a separate adventure. I had not yet reached the point of focusing on one victim and developing a fully detailed plan over an extended period. Nor had I come to the point of expanding the sexual acts involved beyond what I was accustomed to imagining. Also, during this developmental period, I still tended to see the victim as predominately willing. I had not reached the point of envisioning forced activity or the use of any form of physical restraints.

As time went on, my fantasies became increasingly more detailed, to the point of working out precise setting, time, and even invented dialogues. I would lay there in the dark and attempt to imagine every possible reaction that I might encounter from a potential prey and then work out a reply or alternative for all of his hesitations and objections. As a result of this exercise, I began to understand the necessity of manipulating not just the primary victim but also a variety of other people in order to set the victim up. I also realized that by means of exact planning, I could drastically reduce potential problems.

Somewhere around eleven I began to use fantasies as plans, and in doing so, I was amazed at the results. It suddenly felt as if I if I were living in a world that was under my control, a world where I was always one step ahead of other people.

My initial attempts at converting fantasies were not overly involved, and not every attempt worked out exactly as I had planned it. But the degree of success I encountered, and the ease of accomplishing it, mixed together with the incredible thrill of feeling in total control, added a totally new high to my disturbed world. As with just about everything else in my life, as soon as I began this type of activity, I also began escalating it. Each small success ended, not with just a feeling of accomplishment, but also with a heightened appetite for more. By thirteen, I had converted my life into one massive "game" of fantasizing and then working to make my fantasy come true.

At this time, I was increasingly aware of my ability to fantasize about anything, reduce it to a workable plan, eliminate what obstacles I discovered, and then use that perfected plan for obtaining my desired objective in real life. While the initial use of this technique was for sexual purposes, it didn't take long before I was using the same approach to address other aspects of my life. I made it a practice, for the rest of my life, first to reduce a real-life situation to fantasy and then to develop a manipulative plan for accomplishing my goal before taking any action. Slowly, I came to believe that I could do just about anything—provided that I dealt with it in this totally controlled fashion. It was also at this point that I discovered that most adults could be manipulated just as easily as children.

The feeling of power and control that this technique provided me was a definite new high, but even with this new tool, I feared dealing with peers and adults. When I was executing a plan, I felt in control, but outside of the tight confines of a set plan, I felt entirely vulnerable. In retrospect, I realize that what I was doing was simply catching an even more vulnerable person off guard and manipulating him to suit my purposes. But to me at that time, a person who viewed himself as a weak, insignificant victim of fate, it made me feel very alive, very clever, and very, very powerful. Although I was spending more and more time in my fantasy world, I was still confining this activity to my nightly bedtime period.

At about thirteen, I again escalated my fantasies. I would now create fantasies at any time and in any place. I became more obsessed with my fantasies and made them longer and longer.

I found it easier to lose myself in my distorted thoughts,

regardless of the circumstances around me. This new type of fantasy did not end with either masturbation or sleep. The obsession with the imagined victim and situation remained. As soon as I would return to fantasies, I would return to the "unfinished" concept and continue building it from where I had left off.

If I had begun to escape into a mental fantasy world at the age of five or six, by the age of thirteen, I was willingly entering a state that eventually bordered on total obsession and a virtual disassociation with reality. Much later in my life, I did reach the point where I virtually ceased to be functional, but that degree of obsession was a rarity for me. What took place was a slow and constant progression, one in which I spent more and more time lost in my own distorted dreams. I could, and usually did, function on what appeared to be a reasonably normal level, but between tasks, school, work, etc., I increasingly turned from the realities of the real world to the pleasures of my escalating fantasies.

The high in all of this was not just getting the final sexual gratification but getting it according to an increasingly precise plan. In these early years, I was already discovering that while I loved the ultimate sexual act, the real thrill lay in the planning, a thrill that equaled that of the final sexual release. Another thing I was discovering was that for me to deviate from my established plan significantly detracted from my sense of excitement and enjoyment.

For the rest of my adult life outside of prison, my life evolved around my maintaining a "front" for the world to see, while beneath that facade, I was spending increasingly more time inventing fantasies that I acted out. During these mid-teen years, my escalation was confined to setting up different victims and different manipulations to use on them. My fantasies had become real planning sessions, but they had not yet reached the totally obsessive, minutely detailed level that later became the norm of my life.

With the onset of my teens, a period that requires more in the way of developing social contacts, I worked harder at refining my surface cover and became more and more a resident of my own fantasy world. At fifteen, I increased the amount of time I spent wrapped in fantasy and the number of victims I was both using in fantasies and actually abusing. I also continually added a wider and wilder variety of physical settings and physical acts to my imaginings.

After a couple of years of practicing converting my fantasies into realities, I was at a point where I felt entirely in control of the sexual arena.

At fifteen, my life in the real world was a real mess, but apparently one that I covered up well enough that nobody seemed to notice. My relations with everyone around me, regardless of who they were, were cold, distant, and distrustful. Although I had not been subjected to any form of threat, I felt exposed and endangered. I stayed in a totally defensive mode in my dealings with others.

Looking back, it seems that by my teens, I had clearly divided the world into two pieces, me ... and them. Everyone else was either a potential enemy or just another thing to be used in my game, just another piece on the playing board. Instead of doing what all adolescents must eventually do in order to develop into whole, healthy adults—confronting their fears and finding their place in the world around them, I found it easier and more exciting to retreat into my self-centered world of twisted fantasies and to act them out. It was also around fifteen that I first began to envision sadistic elements in my fantasies.

In these new fantasies, I still pictured myself initially setting my victim up by means of verbal manipulation, but now I also fantasized about tying with ropes, or in some other way incapacitating my prey. The big difference between these fantasies and all previous ones was that the entire concept of "consensuality" was discarded. From this time forth, many of my fantasies were built around the initial setup of placing a victim in a position where he was totally helpless. And these new feelings of increased power and control added a thrill that I had never experienced before and one for which I developed an insatiable appetite.

The links between our fantasies and our actions seem to be a very common element among pedophiles and an incredibly dangerous one. For the rest of my life, I continually increased both my fantasies and my offenses, chasing that ultimate high, and like all addicts, never achieving my goal.

We pedophiles want to refuse to accept responsibility for our actions. We want to rationalize a justification for our doing precisely what we want so we try to assure ourselves that fantasizing about an imaginary victim is far, far better than actually abusing a victim. I, myself, and many others whom I have talked with, have frequently assured ourselves prior to, or during a fantasy, that what we were envisioning is something that "we would never do" in real life. Ultimately, however, we become so totally obsessed with the thrill of this new idea that we abandon our commitment to just fantasize, and we act out.

# CHAPTER ELEVEN

## *Amy:*
# Fantasy as a Vehicle for Denial

My mother has had to live in a world of fantasy for as long as I've known her. To her, our family was a "wonderful family," as she would often remind us. (We certainly did need reminding.) My father was "not really an alcoholic." Her optimistic, wishful thinking was contagious. It helped me (as a child) think that things in our house weren't so awful after all.

Gradually, after we had all grown and left home, she began to realize that our family was indeed severely troubled. Not one out of her five adult children was able to sustain a happy, committed relationship with an intimate partner. And my father's alcoholism led to his arrest for a DWI followed by a period of probation.

Yet my mother's deeply ingrained unrealistic thinking kept her (up until a few months before this book's publication) in the marriage, living with and taking care of my abuser, who in turn maintained his alcoholism. As a victim of emotional abuse from my father, she was not able to expend the emotional energy to investigate her life in order to facilitate changes.

Her situation was not unlike mine in that we each put someone else's comfort and happiness ahead of ours. A few years ago I married my second husband, a man who was my direct opposite in most ways. I was clearly a Type A personality; he was almost a hippie, very mellow and slow paced. I was compulsively neat; he was comfortable in a very relaxed, laissez-faire environment. He used substances to alter his mood on a daily basis, and I had a neurotic, fear-based aversion to substances like alcohol and pot. I feared that if I used them, I would lose control of my thinking and being.

Our work ethics were diametrically opposed. I stayed on a treadmill most of my life, feeling that I must always be productive in order to be a worthwhile person, and he was secure enough to feel comfortable working a minimum number of hours a week in order to support himself. Supposedly opposites attract, and they initially did in this relationship. But then my fantasy took over, and I couldn't see our very real, problematic differences. Instead, I could only focus on the fact that not long before we met he had had a serious bout with cancer and had almost lost his life.

I felt it was my duty to help him live the happy life he so deserved. This dissociated thinking was very similar to that of my mother. Extricating myself from this marriage was extremely difficult. I felt that if he ever, God forbid, had a relapse of the cancer, it would be entirely my fault for bringing so much grief and stress in his life.

The fantasy bubble that buoyed my confidence during our engagement burst soon after we married. I realized that a trait of mine that had always been present to some extent in the past had revealed itself on a whole new, intensified level. Now I had married someone with whom I didn't even feel compatible, someone with whom I couldn't even visualize having children, which had always been a much-desired dream of mine.

I was in essence reliving my mother's life by marrying a man for what I perceived to be *his* good, rather than for my own happiness. An example of my failure to see the reality of the situation happened shortly after we were married. We witnessed a drowning at a lake, and despite my attempts to save the swimmer, I couldn't. I waited too long before plunging into the water. I had rationalized from the shore that she wasn't really drowning, despite children's shouts to the contrary. My momentary failure to see the reality of the situation kept me from jumping in immediately when we spotted her distress.

Those few moments of fantasy may have cost a life. Was this an experience I needed to apply to my marriage? How could it not be? Again, I reentered therapy in order to understand what I had done by putting myself in a drowning marriage. My individual therapy and our couples' therapy gave little hope for being able to create a happy marriage and we soon separated and then divorced. It was almost unbearably difficult to put my needs first and to cause another so much pain. The guilt I experienced was almost overwhelming, and for the only time in my life, I needed medication to manage my depression. It stabilized my emotional state enough so that I could move out, continue working, and move on.

I cannot say that I'm "cured" of putting everyone else's needs ahead of mine, but I no longer feel the need to be in therapy, and six months of antidepressants certainly helped me make healthy, life-changing decisions. I'll always struggle with acknowledging my needs and learning to respond to them appropriately, yet I consider myself so much more "healed" than I ever would have thought possible. I am now generally able to view my life and my relationships in a realistic light. My fantasy thinking tends to be by choice and not an automatic coping device, and for this, I can say I've not just survived my abuse, but I've thrived.

I asked Alan if he feels he's "cured" of his pedophilia, after more than a decade of incarceration and prison treatment. He responded in a recent letter: "No, I'm not cured, and I seriously doubt that my resolve, will power, and control would be as stable were there young boys in here, but I have managed to bring my fantasy life under control. The first reaction, the immediate triggering of my sexuality, is still very much there and will most likely always be a problem, but I have at least developed enough internal resources to end the cycle as quickly as it begins.

"In the past two years, I have maintained almost perfect control as far as fantasy and masturbation goes. That may not seem like an earth-shattering accomplishment to anyone else, but I see it as pretty important. From the time that I was about seven to the time that I approached fifty, I never went to sleep without first engaging in some form of actual sexual activity or fantasy accompanied by masturbation. Well, initially there were a lot of restless nights and a lot of making myself get up, turn on the light, and have a cigarette until I regained my control, but the pattern is broken. I can now simply head to bed, read a book, and eventually put it down and sleep without even focusing on fantasy."

Fantasy can be a powerful vehicle for denial, and although it can play a healthy role in the lives of healthy people, it does little to help either the victims or the perpetrators of sexual abuse. When fantasy becomes the basis for one's whole pattern of living, it can only lead one down a secretive path of destruction.

# CHAPTER TWELVE

# *Amy:*

# **Secrets**

As I worked with Alan, I kept my own history of sexual abuse a secret from him. This decision was not unusual. As is typical in most professional therapeutic relationships, I do not share my private life with my patients. However, after years of correspondence, long after our music therapy sessions were finished, it became clear to me that I was doing an injustice both to Alan and myself by not being open about my victimization.

I wrote to him about it and wondered what type of response he would have. He wrote back immediately and showed compassion. He also showed little surprise since he felt I had always understood sexual abuse so well.

It was a major turning point in our relationship when he asked me to write to his cousin's daughter, who had been sexually abused by a family member. I did write, offering her support and reading materials and sharing ideas about various paths for healing. In Alan's writings over the next few years, he often referred to my history when it was pertinent. He once wrote that it made sense to him that I had "been the one to break through my [Alan's] resistance" since I knew "from whence I [he] came."

The much more difficult task for me was telling my family about my book and dealing with their resistance to my decision to write my story. I spoke to and wrote letters to all of them explaining the book and stating that although I was not out to cause embarrassment or pain (and would not use my maiden name), I felt a need to speak openly about our family. With the exception of my mother, it is virtually impossible to engage most of my family in any type of lengthy dialogue about my sexual abuse; they seem to prefer to keep the past as unspoken as possible.

Writing this book was originally fraught with difficult decisions about what to divulge and what to keep private. Yet I could not write a book about the damage caused by keeping secrets and simultaneously not reveal my secret. So, although I felt I risked losing the family I was born into, not keeping any secrets in this book was necessary and something important enough to risk that loss.

Years ago our society wouldn't allow someone to speak openly about a family member having cancer for fear of embarrassment or shame. It was kept a secret. Now we speak freely about this disease without attaching a stigma. Although cancer afflicts people blamelessly, while sexual abuse involves a purposeful attack, in past generations, victims of both were shunned by much of society. My hope is that in the future, we will look back in a similarly compassionate way on the victims of sexual abuse as we now do with cancer patients.

Children who have been abused sexually rarely speak up about their abuse spontaneously. They feel ashamed and keep it a secret. This secret can destroy their spirit. A pedophile, like any other wrongdoer, wants and needs this secrecy. To view secrecy as something only to prevent detection, arrest, and imprisonment is to seriously understate the multifarious role of secrecy in pedophilia. To understand the victim's helplessness, we must understand all aspects of the role of secrecy.

When I was nine years old, my grandfather died unexpectedly. He passed away at the home my family shared with him and my grandmother. As my father told my siblings and me that our grandfather had died, he wept. It was the first time I had ever seen him cry. That evening, as the adults returned from making the preliminary funeral arrangements, I did something quite unusual. Instead of initiating my nightly resistance before being put to bed, I took it upon myself to make my own bedtime arrangements. I quietly bathed myself and dressed in what I knew was my grandfather's favorite pair of baby-doll pajamas. Although it was barely dusk, I lie down in bed, awaiting a visit from his son, my father. Generally I would lie in fear of the dark and the possible visit. Yet, on this particular night, I lay awaiting his visit. I felt it was my duty—my obligation, to make him feel better.

To this day, I don't recall if my father even came into my room or whether he sexually abused me that particular night. I only remember the event as significant because I deliberately put myself in a situation I did not wish to be in, solely to make my father feel better. I sacrificed myself.

All the implications of my behavior were a secret from the rest of the household. No doubt my mother was surprised at the lack of fuss I put up about going to bed that night, but she most likely attributed it to sadness at the loss of my grandfather. Looking back now, my mother realizes that there were signs of my grandfather's sexual interest in me. At the time, those signs were too vague and discreet for her to decipher. And I was convinced that it was a secret that could never be told, because I felt, at nine years old, that there was no one to rescue me.

I did try, in childish ways, to divulge the secret. At one point during that year, I asked my mother to read a book I had just finished because the main character in it was "just like me." She complied, but she was horrified that such a book (*The Bluest Eye* by Toni Morrison) was allowed to be in our elementary school library since it contained graphic details of sexual abuse. It didn't occur to her that this was my way of trying to share my horrible secret with her.

During this time, I was exhibiting several physical symptoms. I had mysteriously contracted severe psoriasis. When I first asked my mother to examine my head, she was completely stunned that huge patches of it covered my entire scalp. There was even more alarm when a physician discovered that my genital area was also affected. Today such a discovery would warrant the attention of agencies for detecting child abuse, and the physician would be mandated to report such a case. However, this 1960s dermatologist's interrogation was limited to a querying raised eyebrow, directed at my mother.

I was also having difficulty following instruction in class, was found masturbating in school on a number of occasions, and feigned mysterious illnesses on a regular basis. It was no surprise that I was unable to continue on to the next grade in school. Although my schoolwork was satisfactory, it was decided by the school and my family that I needed to repeat the year in order to be more emotionally secure. I changed to another neighborhood school in order to repeat without embarrassment, which constituted another disruption in this already traumatic time of my life.

At that time, my mother was not able to see my father's alcoholism, let alone his predatory sexual behavior toward me. Secrets were commonplace in my mother's verbal relationship with my father whenever we children were concerned. When they married, having children had not been discussed because my mother had been told she was "not supposed to be able to have children" by her physician. My father never shared parenting but was financially supportive. Although having children made him "look good," and he kept up a facade of being a "family man," extra expenses were quite upsetting to him. When the price of a gallon of milk went up, my mother needed to finesse the household budget, cutting corners in other areas when she went grocery shopping, rather than tell him about the increase. Keep in mind that our family lived in an affluent upper-middle-class neighborhood and that my father's occupation was well compensated.

Extra childhood expenses such as piano lessons and instruments provoked my father's anger even more and often had to be kept secret between mother and child. Similarly, my mother had to steal her time away from my father if she needed or wished to attend to one of us and she had to rely on white lies in order to be available to us. My father insisted that my mother prepare martinis for him and watch him while he read the newspaper each night.

We usually ate dinner before he came home in order to allow him some quiet and some privacy with my mother in the evening time. When I dared to trespass on this time to ask for a bit of time from my mother, he would often greet me with disdain. He would interrogate me, asking what was so important that I needed to see her. I would be too embarrassed to admit that I just wanted to be near her for a few moments and would construct a more important-sounding answer, like that I needed her to sign my school papers.

Witnessing their relationship gave me what I termed "negative role models" for a marriage that I have consciously striven to avoid. I try to keep no secrets between my husband and me. But keeping a balance between disclosure and secrecy regarding my sexual abuse has been a struggle for me as an adult since the time I started to remember my own history. I am loath to disclose that such a thing ever happened to me because I don't want to be seen as a damaged person.

I also don't want to perpetuate a secret when the situation calls for openness. For example, in my early thirties, I had a few dates (after my divorce from my first husband) with a man slightly older than myself. He, too, was a musician and had also recently come out of a marriage. The important difference between us was that his marriage ended with his wife's suicide.

Because our few dates included improvising music together, our level of intimacy was greater than if we had just done the usual dating thing: dinner and movies. During our music making, he revealed that his wife had left a journal detailing why she felt it necessary to take her own life. She left him to discover her body. Her suicide was in large part due to the sexual abuse she had suffered at the hands of her father when she was a young woman.

During the couple of years after his wife's suicide, he dated another woman who was very young and emotionally fragile. She too was suffering from childhood sexual abuse. Her fits of depression forced her to remain in bed much of the day. As we played together, he told me about these women with tremendous sadness, stating that he would never again date anyone who had ever been sexually abused.

I told him that he was doing just that with me, and then I angrily let him know that by taking that stance he was ruling out more than a quarter of the women in our country as eligible partners.

In the mental health world, one often finds that counselors who work in alcohol and chemical dependency have previously been addicts themselves. Their own histories are not kept secret. On the contrary, they are held up as inspiration, and their past gives credibility to their efforts in helping others with similar issues. But the idea of a therapist referencing his or her own history of sexual abuse while working with a patient is frowned upon. Such a practice is thought to be evidence of a lack of professionalism. The irony is that sexual abuse is forced on victims, not chosen. What is the taboo that accompanies sex abuse? Is it ignorance? Is it the topic of sex itself? Whatever the reason, secrecy is the pervasive rule when speaking of sexual abuse, and the rule serves no one.

As parents, we find it difficult to achieve a comfortable balance concerning our children's privacy. What information do we need to have about their thoughts, attitudes, and behaviors in order not only to keep them safe but also to raise happy and well-adjusted youngsters? Do we pry and meddle into their personal lives? Do we demand to know what they do every waking hour? Which secrets do we ourselves keep from them, and which do we divulge? How do we respond when they do allow us into their confidence? Here are some things I've learned over my years of working with sexual abuse victims regarding secrecy:

- Give affirming or mirroring types of responses when your child first brings you into his or her confidence ("That must have felt horrible when he said that to you") instead of judgmental retorts ("He's right"), statements of blame ("What did you do that made him say that?"), or—the most common error among parents—unsolicited advice ("What you need to do is ..."). This will enable the youngster to speak more freely about whatever is on his or her mind.

- Consider the secrets you keep from your own child and know that she or he is probably aware of them anyway. Ask yourself why you maintain them and whom you are really protecting. Consciously decide if it is absolutely necessary to keep these secrets. I grew up witnessing my mother angrily slamming cupboard doors as she prepared meals and asking her, "What's wrong" and hearing, "Nothing."

  Her words certainly didn't match her actions, and this incongruence made me feel unsafe and guilty. Even if she couldn't have told me why she was angry, it would have been helpful for her to say something to the effect of "I'm very angry now about something that is not your fault. I'll be able to work it out on my own and be in a better mood later."

- Investigate the ramifications of asking your child to keep secrets. Even seemingly innocuous secrets can have harmful results ("Don't tell your sister that we stopped for ice cream," which makes your child wonder what you may be keeping from him or her).

- Try to ask open-ended questions in order to get more information when your child speaks ("What happened then?" instead of "Did he do it then?").

- Be aware of your body position during dialogues with your youngster. Are your arms folded across your chest? This exhibits a lack of openness. Are you towering over the child? This gives him or her a feeling of powerlessness. Putting yourself in an open, non-threatening light will enable your child to be more honest with you.

- Examine your home environment in order to foster opportunities to communicate with your family.

  One of the saddest things I've heard in the locker room at my gym was a conversation between two mothers of young teens. One woman was a teacher at her son's school and did not want his friends to see her in her home environment without makeup, perhaps engaged in less-than-desirous positions such as being a "couch potato," or in her shorts.

  Whatever the reasons, she was uncomfortable having his friends in her immediate home environment, so she created a basement room for him. She happily described the elements to his room—access from the outside without coming through the main part of the house, separate phone, TV and computer, and even a separate refrigerator and bathroom. This mother was thrilled that both she and her son could maintain their private lives under the same roof.

  I listened, thinking she now had cut off access to knowing who her son's friends are, what they are like, when they are over, what he watches on TV, and who he talks with on the phone. She cut off opportunities to get to know her son. All I could think of was the grave risk into which she was putting her son by abdicating parental attention to his life. How could he be honest with her if he wasn't even around her? We must examine our priorities and levels of comfort and think about the price our selfishness takes on our children's emotional health.

It is crucial that we use just as many positive techniques to enable our children to be honest with us as the molester employs negative ones in order to snare his prey. *Secrecy is the crux of sexual abuse. Without it, there could be no abuse.*

Open, honest communication is the single-most powerful tool we have as parents in protecting our children from pedophiles. Really listen to how you speak to youngsters, even try tape-recording a mealtime and analyzing it later to see what kinds of verbal interactions you most often make. Determine if they are the sorts of phrases that invite open communication.

- Practice patterns of verbalization that will encourage openness.

- Ask for feedback from your family and other close acquaintances about your communication style, and explain why it's important that you actively investigate it.

- Help your children understand that in order for them to feel more comfortable with you, you need to more fully connect with and get to know them.

# CHAPTER THIRTEEN

*Alan:*

# Using Secrets to Entice and Ensnare

For me, secrecy was the glue that held my fantasies together. Secrecy was the element that added a feeling of excitement, heightening the overall thrill I got from offending. It represented a twisted sense of personal power and personal worth, and ultimately it was my critical weapon both to entice and ensnare my young victims.

Just about everybody can remember a time when small secrets, such as who was getting what for Christmas or a birthday, were exciting and important elements in our limited lives. In childhood, having a secret was the ultimate status symbol. It added a feeling of importance, prestige, and the sense of being in control. Fortunately for most people, the allure of secrets is something they outgrow. For many of us, however, the fascination with secrets continues to be a major part of our lives.

I am also reasonably confident that most of us, if we are totally honest with ourselves, admit that we have a continuous need for care and attention. Children have an insatiable need for care and attention, and pedophiles frequently use that need to abuse them. I combined the mysterious allure of secrecy with large portions of attention in order to draw my young victims into my trap. My methods were not quick but designed to build, very slowly, a child's acceptance of the need for secrets. At the same time, secrecy gave me the opportunity to make a child believe that I was the only person in the world who really cared for him and looked out for him.

I confess that until recently, I didn't look too carefully at the role of secrecy in my life. I understood that I maintained a tight screen of secrecy to cover my activities and avoid being caught, but I have begun to see that my secrets, and more particularly my need and love of them, tell a great deal about how I saw myself and the world surrounding me. Most of the self-confident, self-sufficient, and stable adults I have known didn't seem to have a need for secrets in their lives. While there was information that they didn't want to make public, the possession of these secrets didn't provide them with any sense of excitement or personal power.

I am of the opinion that the adults who continue to need and desire secrets are those who feel that their own lives lack any real interest, worth, or excitement. These people, of whom I was always one, appear to use secrets as a means of increasing their own self-respect, and supporting their own deflated egos. Seeing adults today who are still using secrets to support their existence always brings to my mind an image of an angry child standing in the middle of a playground attempting to save face in some situation by yelling out, "Oh yeah, well I know something that you don't know!!!!!"

As a pedophile, I feel that I used secrecy in two different but interrelated ways. I initially used secrecy to entice my victims into getting close to me and ultimately to ensnare them into compliance and silence. And I used secrecy as a way of avoiding punishment as seen in the next chapter.

As I mentioned, I usually only attempted to molest a child after getting to know the potential victim and his family. Once I gained access to that circle, I would attempt to gain as complete an understanding of the boy as I could, see how he related to the adults and other family members, and if it appeared that there was a realistic possibility of success, I would then begin to groom my target. If I had determined that this child did not have the type of personality that led him always to discuss things with his parents, I knew that reluctance to communicate on his part could be developed into the keeping of secrets.

Although I tailored my approach to suit the individual victim, the overall process seldom varied. First I would test the boy in some simple fashion to see if he had the ability to keep a secret. In doing this, I would usually, when we were alone, make some intended mistake. I would, for example, swear in front of him. Having done this, I would explain that I should not have and ask him to keep my mistake just between the two of us.

I would also be careful to point out that the reason for not telling his parents was that if they worried about my being a bad influence on him, he might not be allowed to spend time with me, and then we couldn't enjoy going to the video arcades or to whatever other activities I knew he enjoyed.

In this initial step I wanted to make the boy see the keeping of secrets as just something that we did to keep us together and to keep both of us out of any trouble. When he assured me that he wouldn't tell, I would make sure to reward him with some simple thing, like going bowling or fishing, and make sure that he felt trusted and "grownup" because this adult was dealing with him on a different level.

Having taken his small first step, I waited to see if he did, in fact, keep quiet about the incident. If he didn't, I might have created some small suspicion on his parent's part, but I was not in any real trouble. I would then immediately end all attempts at victimizing him. On the other hand, if after a week or so it was clear that this secret had been kept, I once again rewarded the child, explaining why he was being rewarded and continued with the escalation of the process.

For the next few weeks or months, I would spend every available opportunity subtly drawing the child closer and closer. I would constantly tell him how special he was, how grown-up he was, and how all of us needed to find someone in life whom we could really trust. I always portrayed his parents as concerned people, but people who really had no choice except to put limits on him because they were his parents.

I was careful not to attack his parents but rather to slowly change how he looked at them. A very large part of this initial grooming process was to establish a connection in the child's mind between parental authority and the desirability of secrets that could outmaneuver that unwanted intrusion on his freedom.

Virtually every boy I have ever met has the same conflicting emotions regarding the role of parents in his developing world, and I attempted to exploit this frustration and anger. By slowly getting the child to view secrets as a necessary means of protecting something that he enjoyed, I laid the foundation for a mountain of escalating secrets, all of which were designed to entrap the child as a sexual victim.

As time passed, having met with success in the keeping of smaller secrets, I gradually increased the importance of the secrets and the rewards for keeping them. I would, for example, let the boy know that I didn't object to his having some of my beer or smoking while at my house ... but, for his sake as well as my own, we obviously couldn't let "them," or anybody else, know about it.

What I was doing, of course, was creating a mental environment where the victim began to see his potential victimizer as the person in the world who trusted him and cared for him the most. Secrets became proof of our mutual trust, and I worked at getting the child to be totally open with me about everything in life. I got him to tell me what his parents said about me and what questions they might be asking him, carefully coaching him on how to avoid their attempts to break us up and limit his freedom. I needed to get him to the point where he knew that if he really wanted his parents to let him do something he could always count on me to try to get them to give in. Little by little, all of his possible reservations and inhibitions were shed, and he began to come to me with every complaint, question, and request. In most cases, the victim would call me to discuss how to handle his parents when he wanted to do something they might not normally allow. He began to rely on my being there to act as his friend, mentor, advocate, and ally.

Throughout this entire period, which might well take up to a year, I continued to draw him further and further away from trusting his parents and worked toward his ultimately seeing them as a necessity but one to be outwitted and controlled. Also, through this period, I worked to create an atmosphere in which whatever we did or said to each other was kept strictly between us.

I allowed the child almost total freedom when we were alone, and after a reasonable amount of time, and a heightened degree of my confidence in his ability to keep his mouth shut, I started moving into the sexual arena. At first it was just a few offhand remarks and off-color jokes, but as he got comfortable with the openness of sexual talk, I moved to letting him know that some soft-core pornographic material was in the house and that he was old enough to see it. Still, I made no quick jump into either sexually disturbing conversations or physical contact. At this stage, I just wanted the child to see this new area as one more needed secret and to accept it as just a routine part of his present life.

Very shortly after introducing magazines and sexual talks, I would set it up so that he could view a hard-core porno film. Again, I made off-color remarks and even went so far as to discuss the reality of this type of material causing a man to get erected, but I didn't press the issue. When the secret was kept, which I was confident it would be, I used our next opportunity to allow him (make him) view a more hard-core film, and this time I was more specific about the physical effects that this type of viewing had on me. I would quickly point out that he probably wasn't old enough yet to be stirred by this (which was a real challenge to his young ego), and he would feel (in most cases) compelled to defend his manhood by assuring me that he also enjoyed this and got stimulated by it. Again, I didn't push but just complimented him on being so mature for his age and the way that nothing seemed to bother him.

My primary concern at this stage was not his telling his parents, for I was pretty sure he would not go home and talk about drinking, smoking, or watching pornography, but rather his trying to impress one of his friends by telling him about it and thus possibly exposing my actions. I carefully instructed him as to the dangers of sharing this information with anyone, and he repeatedly assured me that he was not about to risk losing what he had.

Now that he had continued to accept the drinks, smokes, and various rewards I offered and now that he had come back repeatedly to watch porno films, the secrets that he was keeping were beginning to become virtually impossible for him to violate, at least in his young mind. How could he, for example, explain to his parents that he not only allowed me to give him beer, cigarettes, trips, money, etc., and to do virtually anything he wanted to and also that he regularly reported on what they thought and said, without clearly implicating what he now saw as his guilt in our actions?

Keeping all of these seemingly minor secrets had built up a feeling of equal responsibility and equal guilt in this totally innocent child, something I had worked to achieve, and it was this inability to inform on me without having to explain his own willing participation that finally kept him captive to my sick desires.

As soon as I worked him through the shock and confusion of an initial fondling attack, I did everything in my power to get the child to submit to performing a sexual act on me. I normally tried to get the child to engage in oral sex quickly, as I knew that once he had willingly agreed to do this for a given reward, he would be in a position where telling was almost impossible for him. Now, even if he did want to tell his parents that things were wrong, he felt that he would have to tell them about his perverted sexual behavior, and I had already made him sure that if anybody else ever saw this, they would never understand. The confusion and emotional conflict was simply too heavy for him to see a way out, and so he normally fell back on the established pattern of just accepting what happened, finding some type of consolation in being allowed to pick his own rewards, and keeping the entire affair secret for his own sake.

Once a child realized that he couldn't tell without incriminating himself, he usually gave up any type of resistance to my further suggestions regarding sexual activities. At this point, his spirit was broken, and he was mentally resigned to doing what I had carefully groomed him to do—to disassociate the real him from these "crazy acts."

It was during this later period that I kept telling the victim that everybody in life ends up doing things that they don't really enjoy, that's part of life, but as long as you get something out of it in the end, you win. Normally, beyond this point there was no reluctance or resistance on the victim's part.

## CHAPTER FOURTEEN

*Alan:*

# Secrecy as a Means of Avoiding Punishment

This next application of secrecy in my life is the one that I think most people will find easy to comprehend. In using a blanket of secrets to cover up my illegal activities, I was no different from any other individual who wished to avoid public disclosure and potential punishment.

I would rarely pick up a strange child, especially in the area near my home city, for fear of accidentally encountering him later. Prior to my taking the first physical action against a victim, I would have spent a great deal of time getting to know both the child and his family. Before I reached the point of physically committing myself to this crime, I wanted to make sure that it was as close to foolproof as I could make it and that the victim was groomed as well as possible to keep our secret.

Despite all of the years in which I practiced and developed this method, and my careful selection and grooming of the potential victim, when I first committed a physical act with a child, I was always scared out of my mind. Having now taken the step beyond words, I felt totally vulnerable, exposed, and threatened. What I needed at this instant was some means of assuring myself that the victim was going to remain silent.

Now I went from being obsessed with committing the abuse to being obsessed with defusing what I saw as a highly explosive situation. But having been through this situation hundreds of times, I worked out an approach to deal with the victim and my own feelings of anxiety and fear. Although the approach differed with each victim, the overall pattern remained similar and went something like this:

## POINT ONE:
### Determine the emotional impact on the victim.

Immediately following the initial act, I needed to determine just what effect it had on the child's mental state. Over the years, I had seen postmolestation reactions ranging from seeming indifference to total fear, confusion, and tears. My first concern was to figure out the boy's present mood and find a way of defusing the immediate impact of what he had just been subjected to. Under no circumstances was I going to take the child home until I had the opportunity to do everything in my power to control the situation.

## POINT TWO:
### Attempt to get the victim to minimize the crime and see it as a "once-in-a-lifetime" mistake.

In this regard, I treated virtually every victim the same. As soon as the initial act was done, I would begin to say repeatedly, "I never should have done this" and that "it would never, ever happen again." As I used drinking alcohol as a prop in almost every initial action, I told the child that I must have had too much, that I was terribly sorry.

Despite the devastating impact of this introduction to perverted sexual activity, almost every victim saw me as being tremendously upset for what I had done, enormously concerned for their feelings, and totally remorseful for having made a serious "mistake." In this regard, I used the child's natural instinct to love and forgive in order to shift his attention from his own victimization to my obvious regret for having done something that bothered him.

With almost every victim this ploy was successful, and very quickly he was assuring me that it was all right, persuading me that he was willing to forgive my error and that I didn't have to worry about his getting me into trouble. When the child reached this point of role reversal, I began to employ the next manipulation.

### POINT THREE:
**Introduce the element of large-scale rewards for the victim's being "such a special person."**

In answer to the child's assurances that he understood it was just an alcohol-induced error in judgment, I would begin telling him how much I appreciated his understanding, and how very special and grown-up he was to be able to see things in that light. I would be very careful here to explain that not just any kid was likely to be as mature, understanding, and considerate. What I wanted to instill within him at this juncture was the feeling that telling anyone about what had happened would make him ordinary instead of special.

At this stage, I manipulated the victim to begin to think that this ability of his to deal with whatever happened, and to not make a big deal out of it, was something that made him a trusted, respected, and special friend. As he could not envision my ever making this type of mistake again, particularly when I was so clearly devastated by having done it, he felt safe in making the promise to "keep this just between the two of us."

Once the child had begun to feel sorry for me and to work toward assuring me that things were all right, I would respond by playing on both his ego and greed. After repeated thanks and assurances from him, I would make it appear that I suddenly came up with the idea of rewarding this outstanding act of friendship and understanding. I would point out that I had just planned on taking him home, but that because he was so special and so cooperative, we needed to do something equally special for him.

Then I would suggest some major activity that I knew that he was dying to do but wouldn't normally have a chance to do. I would suggest that we spend the rest of the day skiing, slot-car racing, or doing whatever other activity would thrill him. Despite their attempts to assure me that it wasn't necessary, most victims usually quickly gave in to their desires to do something special, and we would head off. For the rest of the day, I would spare no expense in showering the child with every possible reward (but nothing that he would take home with him or have to explain to his parents). I intentionally encouraged him to go totally beyond the normal level of his desires, insisting that because of what he had done, he was entitled to anything. I wanted to hear him begin to say things such as "it really wasn't that bad, and it really didn't bother me too much." Once he began to verbalize in this manner, I would react by again increasing the praise and rewards, and by slowly introducing the next phase of the manipulation.

## POINT FOUR:
Make the victim see that he is not the only one and that

**one other special friend learned to benefit from being cooperative.**

Once the victim had begun to say these things, I would tell him how great his attitude was and then explain (or hint at) the fact that only once before had I ever met as cooperative and caring a friend. Normally when I had tossed out this small hint, the victim immediately wanted to hear more about this other person.

Now I would invent a former "friend" (usually calling him a cousin). I wouldn't provide much information but just imply that one other boy had proven himself to be as good a friend as he had, explaining that I would never forget just how great this other kid ended up being. Normally it wasn't too long before my current victim was begging me to tell him more, and so I introduced him to the made-up story of my mystery cousin Paul.

I explained that Paul was now grown-up and lived on the West Coast, but that when he was younger, he and I used to spend a lot of time together. I also explained that on one occasion we had been camping, and I had had a bit too much to drink, and "… well, I did to him the same type of thing that we did this afternoon." At this point, I would pause, as if I had completed telling my story, and without exception, each victim wanted to know how Paul reacted and what happened next.

After some prodding on the victim's part, I agreed to tell him about it. I then described Paul as being a little older than this victim but in all other aspects being very similar. I explained what activities Paul and I enjoyed, nonsexual activities, and always made sure that they were exactly the type of activities that my current victim would want to take part in.

Then I would describe that night, saying that although he

didn't enjoy what I had done, he was willing to forget it. At this point, I introduced the new element to the manipulation. I told him that Paul was very much like him, but that "being a bit older and more adult," he realized that we could both benefit from my mistake. When the current victim asked what he meant, I carefully explained the theory of making deals with each other.

I told him that since Paul was older, having this sort of thing happen didn't really bother him much at all, and that since he knew I would always make it up to him, in the same way that I'm now doing for you, my cousin suggested that it wasn't important. Paul, I pointed out, was a very grown-up and smart kid. He knew that if I got drinking too much, I would do something crazy, and he suggested that as long as I always made him happy, he was willing to put up with my strange games.

Most victims wanted to know if it ever happened again (something they were afraid of), and I seemingly reluctantly confessed that it did, but I quickly pointed out that it did so only when Paul asked for me to do it. Most victims seemed confused with this concept, and I explained that some time after the initial incident, Paul was home alone, bored out of his mind, putting up with his parents who were on his back about everything, when he called me at my house.

He suggested that I talk his parents into letting him spend the night with me, so that we could go fishing or something, and that if I was willing to rescue him, he wouldn't mind it if I, or we both, got a little drunk. I explained to the victim that at first I didn't understand what he meant, but Paul then said that if I was willing to get him out of there and let him have some fun, he was willing to let me make another mistake.

The victim always wanted to know if I went and got him,

and I said I did. But I added that I told him he didn't have to let me do this to him just to have me take him somewhere. We were friends, I pointed out, and I would be more than happy to help him out. I also added that Paul then explained that if we were really friends, we should both be willing to help and trust each other. He said that he knew he didn't have to trade favors with me, but since I was always doing something for him, he wanted occasionally to do something special for me.

The victim was usually very curious at this point and wanted to know if Paul and I continued to do this. And I assured him that we did but only when Paul wanted to, and only when he was willing to let me take him to do something very special.

Usually, after this involved story, during which I continued to point out how much alike this victim and Paul were, the boy reached the point of agreeing that Paul was a good friend and that what he volunteered to do was just proving that he liked me as much as I liked him.

What I had intended to do through this involved process was to:

a. Control the initial impact of this first abuse;
b. Manipulate the situation to get the child to feel sorry for me;
c. Manipulate the child to the point where I felt pretty confident that he wasn't going to inform on me;
d. Provide him with a made-up peer so that he didn't see himself as alone or different;
e. Open the door for his next molestation.

I now viewed the victim as relatively safe to take home, but I still was far from confident or relaxed concerning my exposure. I had done everything within my power to control the situation, but I still felt vulnerable and very anxious concerning the next twenty-four-hour period. Controlling the child while I had him alone was easy, but I worried about his reactions when he got home and was beyond the reach of my manipulations.

That night was terror for me, and I usually spent it alone in my house, expecting every passing car to be the police, or each telephone call to be that of angry parents.

The following day I was still in a hyperstate of anxiety and fear, and nothing would make those feelings abate except for finding a reason to visit the family. Then I could determine for myself that there was no noticeable change in the behavior of the boy or any member of his family. As soon as it was practical, I did precisely that, and when the child greeted me in the customary manner, and the parents behaved in the usual fashion, I relaxed. If the child did not seem to be normal, I would quickly find a reason for getting him off to myself and reinforcing the previous day's grooming (this was almost never required).

There is a saying in most recovery programs to the effect that we are only as sick as our secrets and our need for secrets. Secrets destroy, and the need for the seeming excitement and importance of secrets in our lives clearly points out a very troubled and, I believe, potentially dangerous personality. Today, when I hear someone use the term "innocent secret," I cringe, for there isn't any such entity. Innocence and secrecy are mutually exclusive states, and the only time that they seem to come together is when one is being used to destroy the other.

# CHAPTER FIFTEEN

*Amy:*

# Obsession with Control

We have seen in previous chapters that each facet of the pedophile's obsessive mind-set engenders a complementary feeling in the victim. Every situation that the pedophile designs in order to feel powerful results in a comparable feeling of powerlessness and lack of control in the victim. Often former child victims struggle as adults with issues of control since they were in such powerless situations when they were sexually abused. For each element of control that the pedophile inflicts, the child loses a bit more of his or her sense of strength. While it is generally painful for the reader to learn about how this control is established, it is essential to our understanding of the true meaning of pedophilia.

Both my father and grandfather used control and power to victimize me. Their absolute authority left me completely vulnerable to their manipulations. They made it very clear that I *would* not tell anyone about our relationship. There were no bribes, just the knowledge that I would do as told and never speak of the abuse.

This control was not so different from Alan's in structure. My grandfather, for example, made advances bit by bit, upping the ante each time and giving rewards later, such as letting me choose a puppy. These rewards made me feel more special than my four brothers. His sense of control seemed omnipotent and unquestionable. I had to do as I was told, and there was no other option. The threat, always implicit, was a vital one: If I made my grandfather and father angry or unhappy, it would mean the destruction of the family. And I was not capable of that.

Control in my own life has been of critical importance to me. It has shaped my sense of self and served as an impetus for my personal achievements. My need for control manifested itself largely in a need to control myself. I still struggle with a driving perfectionism and an insistence on over-achievement. My need for control manifests itself in three realms—physical, mental and environmental.

- Physical—I have always been quite athletic, and as I examine my patterns of physical exercise, it is no surprise to me that the areas I selected involved exact movements that are executed in a precise and unchanging order. I was a gymnast as a teenager and a circus performer in my midtwenties, and I currently lift weights. The specific events I selected were the uneven parallel bars as a gymnast and later the trapeze. These events required a great deal of physical strength and control, especially the latter. As a child, I was not able to be in control of my body, so later I gained complete control of every muscle and joint and became as powerful as I could. I also tried to control my physical inner-workings. From the age of thirteen, I never missed a day of school due to illness. High school, college, two graduate programs, and more than a decade of my working career had passed in this way before I finally (on one occasion) took a sick day. Looking back, I think I felt that if I were to succumb to physical illness, I was not in control of my body and was somehow in danger.

- Mental—Many people in my life, including my husband and my closest friends, have been concerned that I push myself too hard in my work. In many of the letters I've received from Alan over the past ten years, he has often urged me to slow down. I've been a hard and diligent worker since I was thirteen. At this age I began living a life that was possible for me to recall in my memory later.

  The age thirteen represented the endpoint of my memory blank. Prior to this age, I was a juvenile delinquent with a police record. I cheated in school, stole from stores, and hung out with a wild group of kids, vandalizing property.

  My family moved quite often due to my father's job and when my family moved for the last time, I saw the path I was on and decided I was going to turn my life around. I was going to learn to play the flute, which I felt was the sound of my soul (I already played the guitar and piano), and I was going to make straight As and meet good kids. In our new city, I performed in bands and orchestras, competed on gymnastic teams, managed swimming pools, lifeguarded and taught swim lessons, led children's choirs, managed a babysitting service, and led an extremely active social life, while making the honor roll in both junior and senior high school.

  My need for mental control continued long after high

school. The summer preceding college, I read an article claiming that humans only need four hours of sleep a night, and I regulated my sleep habits accordingly. This enabled me to complete a lengthy degree in music therapy in a condensed period of time, often taking much more than the normal academic load. I maintained close to a 4.0 GPA while being in several sororities and clubs, holding various offices, dating extensively, and performing as a musician in orchestras, bands, and ensembles.

I felt that I must be in control of my mind at all times, leaving no time for relaxation for fear that my mind would take over and recall more horrific times that I was not yet capable of remembering. It took me many years of healing before I was able to extricate myself from my obsessive need to control my thoughts and actions to such an extreme extent.

- Environmental—As an adult, I have moved several times from state to state in order to pursue various academic degrees from different institutions. Each time I moved, I became more adept at the process of packing and unpacking my possessions. My friends gape in wonder at the expediency I demonstrate in unpacking an entire house in less than a week, down to hanging pictures and planting flowers. In just a few days, my house will look like I've been there for months, without a box in sight. This is just one example of my need to control my exterior environment. Because my inner self has felt so chaotic much of my life, my need to establish the utmost control over what I can surfaces in my home. Everything must be in its place.

These examples serve to illustrate my continuing need to control every aspect of my life. Maintaining control can be beneficial, but ultimately it can also be exhausting and restrictive. A personal goal for the past few years has been to get off the treadmill, relax, and relinquish control. Strangely, it has been easier to do this with the arrival of my children. Being pregnant made my body take on a new identity, and being responsive to and responsible for infants with needs of their own has helped me loosen the controlling grip directing my life.

Alan's testimony that follows illustrates, in detail, how issues of control are at the heart of his and all pedophiles' actions. His rhetoric is almost verbatim from our years of correspondence, and as I have read and reread his writings over such a long period, I have been struck by a fascinating observation. The systems of manipulation and the structure of escalation, including the postponement of his victims' climax, are not just in the subject matter of his testimony. They are in fact actually woven into his writing.

# CHAPTER SIXTEEN

## *Alan:*

# Control

After I was arrested, a doctor who is a leading authority on pedophilia told me that sex really wasn't the driving force behind my perverted actions. At that time, I thought that this was the stupidest statement I had ever heard. I was convinced that everything I had ever done in life had always been centered on what I saw as my uncontrollable perverted sexual desires. As soon as I heard him utter those words, I was angry. I was mad because after all those years of hiding in my twisted world of sexual fantasies and perverted offending, my carefully maintained facade had finally been ripped away, and I was in a position where I could speak honestly and openly with a leading expert. And his answer seemed totally wrong. Was he nuts? How could I have spent my entire life, both as a child and adult, constantly molesting little boys and now have him try to tell me that sex was not really at the root of it all?

Over the years, I've come to understand just how accurate that doctor's remarks were. Anyone who looked at my life might easily believe that all the insanity was nothing more than a pathetic individual's attempts to find some type of perverted sexual gratification. But if you begin to carefully examine the process, to dissect the method by which I went about entrapping my young victims, and the pattern of my actions once I had manipulated a child to the point where he offered little or no resistance to my demands, a very different picture emerges. I am convinced that while there are many factors at work in my choosing to act out, the driving force, the element that triggered and spurred on others, was my insatiable obsession to feel that I had control.

Later, a prison physician wanted to know what my victim and I did when I was not molesting him. When I answered him by saying that there was never a point when I wasn't molesting him, this doctor looked totally confused. His confusion demonstrated what I feel is the major missing piece in most people's understanding of the abuse cycle. Like most people, he viewed what I had done in terms of individual perverted acts over time.

I have been often asked the question, "How could any child be duped to the point where he would not only submit to enduring sexual perversions but continue to allow them to take place over an extended period of time?" I came to realize that the average person thought of abusing in terms of individual incidents and acts, rather than in terms of its being one constant and continual process from beginning to end.

Most critical of all was the unending manipulative dialogue between my victims and myself. Every step in the entire abuse cycle was dependent on my being able to use words to control the child. To control the child's body, I had first to find a way of controlling his mind, and clearly my only means of accomplishing that was through constant verbal assault. But the goal was never just sexual submission. What

I did was orchestrate a crescendo of victim submission leading to the final movement I intended for them. And in this crescendo, each successive note was critically important for its own sake and also for what it provided to the overall dynamic of the complete piece.

From the very outset, control was a primary obsession for me. As I have described, even in very early childhood, I felt threatened and confused by the world surrounding me. I felt very different from other people and very much alone. It was then that I began retreating into my own mental world of fantasies. Not too long after these initial fantasies were created, I discovered the act of sexually stimulating myself, although at that early age, I had no understanding of why masturbation felt good to me. I quickly began linking these two forms of pleasure together, creating endless fantasies centered on this new pleasant physical act. It wasn't long before sexual fantasies weren't enough.

I was seven when I first offended. I lured a boy of five into an old garage that was being used as a storage shed and manipulated him into pulling down both his pants and underpants. It was in the middle of summer, and the child was wearing no shirt, shoes, or socks, so that when he submitted to my demands, he was standing naked before me. Once he had stood there for a moment or two, staring at the floor to avoid my eyes, I told him to get dressed, and after bribing him to keep our secret, we left.

As I look back at this incident, two things are clear to me. First, that I had no physical contact with the boy. But more importantly, I remember that the absolute high came for me at the instant that the child undid the snap to open his pants. I felt as if electricity was pouring through me. I enjoyed making him stand there, but the rest of his act, actually taking the pants down, was not nearly as exciting as when he made the first move indicating that he was going to do what I wanted.

Two other pedophiles in the past few years have related similar tales to me. In one instance, the offender was ten and forced a younger boy to allow himself to be entirely stripped in the seclusion of a basement. The offender recalled removing each piece of clothing and making the child stand in front of him but then telling him to re-dress without any physical contact. When I asked why, in light of the fact that his victim was cooperating, he didn't do more, the man replied, "I guess I had what I wanted, so I just stopped." I then asked what he found exciting about that first offense. At first he said "everything," but when I asked him to be a bit more specific, he said, "Well ... when I started taking his shirt off and he didn't resist ... he didn't even say anything ... I felt so good, I was shaking."

The other pedophile who had a similar initial experience was a young man who was molested from the age of six until he was fourteen. He claimed that before his first offense, he had honestly not dreamed about doing it to anyone else, and he said that it "just seemed to pop into my head that night." While baby-sitting for some married friends' seven-year-old boy, this offender manipulated the child into playing a game of doing dares. He dared the boy to do a variety of small non-sexual tricks and then dared him to take off his pajama top, which the boy did quickly. The dares continued until the boy was naked, and then he was ordered to reclothe himself and sent to bed. With this offender, as with the last, I asked what he found to be exciting about it, and he replied, "When he took the top off, I was pleased but not excited too much. Later, when I dared him to remove the bottoms, knowing that he then would be down to his shorts, he stalled. I mean he looked at me confused. Finally he asked if I was gonna want everything off. I said something like … 'maybe,' and he just stood there. I talked some more, and after a minute or so like that, he began undoing the string. When he did that, I knew I won, I had him, and I was really excited."

When I asked why he didn't carry it further with the child, particularly as he knew how to do every form of perversion from personal experience and admitted that he enjoyed this type of sexual contact, he replied, "I never figured that one out. Later on, not that night … but like a couple months later, I made him do a lot of things, but I guess the important thing on the first night was just making him do it, you know, undress. Once he gave in, I sent him to bed, then went to the john, and jerked off."

In each case the offender made the victim do a specific thing, and in each case once that demand was obeyed the offender stopped. Admittedly, there could be numerous reasons why each of us did not move to the point of physical abuse at that time, but I really believe that it was more a case of our having gratified our immediate sense of needing to prove control. My guess is that we demand compliance to equal the current need we feel for being in control. That is, once we have proven our control sufficiently, we don't demand more. Unfortunately, for many of us, the need to re-prove our "power" becomes more and more constant. And frequently the level of proof we need to validate our sense of control continues to escalate.

In my particular case, this initial success led to my spending many nights fantasizing about the incident. I repictured it in my mind and used it as a stimulus for masturbation. After doing this for a while, however, it lost its thrill. In order to make it more exciting, I didn't just picture what had taken place, but I added to it.

I fantasized about making the boy stand and let me touch him. After fantasizing about this for a short time, working out the place to do it and what to say, etc., I talked the same victim into coming into the building's basement storeroom and molested him again. The difference this time was that watching him take his pants down, although exciting, did not bring back the electric high I'd had earlier. I kept talking to the boy until he agreed to let me touch him, and the minute he shook his head yes, the electricity hit. I don't deny that I found touching him pleasurable, for I did, but the real high was once more when he submitted, and I saw that he was defeated.

What I didn't see at that early age was that each time I felt the thrill that came when a victim gave in to my demands, the thrill quickly left me wanting to have it again. At first I tried to re-create the feeling by having a victim do what he had done before, but it was never the same—pleasurable but not exciting. Every time I proved that I was able to make someone do what I wanted, I found myself having to prove it again, and again, and again.

I also learned that making a new victim do the same act was electric. Now I had two tools for feeling the excitement—finding new victims and making the current victim do something new. I know for a fact that before I turned eight, I was regularly getting new victims to submit and that I had moved from forcing exposure to oral sex. From seven until roughly eleven, I followed the following, set escalating pattern:

1. Target—pick a boy and get him alone.
2. Exposure—force him to expose himself.
3. Touch.
4. Masturbate him.
5. Perform oral sex on him.

6. Get him to masturbate me.
7. Get him to perform oral sex.
8. Target next victim.

The pattern was always the same, although the speed at which each victim progressed through these different stages varied widely. Before I was nine, it was not unusual for me to have several victims in various stages of this pattern at the same time, sometimes molesting them during the same day.

I also discovered that by working out how I would force each new victim into not resisting in fantasies prior to actually trying it, I was always prepared for whatever objection the boy might raise before he raised it. Each new victim taught me a little more about how to control the situation. By nine, I felt that I could get any kid I wanted. But, even though a new victim was always exciting, even adding more and more was losing its real high. And once a victim didn't offer any resistance to whatever I demanded, he wasn't fun anymore. I wanted more.

One of my victims at that time was a seven-year-old who, during the summer, had been abused so frequently that he no longer offered any resistance to demands. As we walked to school one morning, I implemented my latest fantasy. I told him to meet me in the boy's room at a certain time. Up until this time I had only molested a boy when we were in a spot that was totally isolated. The kid really didn't want to have to do it there. He suggested we meet after school and that he'd go to the usual place and be really good, but that wasn't what I was looking for. As we entered the building, I commanded him to be there on time.

He came. He was scared stiff and actually shaking, but he came. And the minute I saw him come through the bathroom door, the electric bolt hit me. I proved I could make him come. He was so shaken, jumping at every little sound in the hall, that I didn't do a thing. I didn't have to, for I had already had my high. I told him to meet me after school and sent him back to class. I knew now that by making even the most submissive of victims submit to abuse in a setting that made the entire act more difficult for him heightened my sense of being in control.

At this point, I didn't figure out a lot of new places for each new victim but pretty much subjected the new victim to the same series of settings that proved difficult for the previous victim. The final step in this rotation was forcing the child to perform sexually in his own house while other family members were in nearby rooms. Once a victim had performed this step, I lost the ability to find new excitements and steadily withdrew from him, going to yet another new victim.

I need to point out that not every boy went along with all of the steps in my cycle. I encountered a lot of victims who permitted me to continue to a certain point and then flatly rejected all attempts beyond that level. This loss of control drove me crazy. I would try every manipulation, bribe, and promise I could fantasize about with those boys, but some of them still would not surrender. When I reached that point, I was frustrated and dropped him for another, more willing victim. But something about this incident fascinated me, and I kept fantasizing about it night after night. This boy, out of his fear for having to perform in this new spot, had practically begged me to let him do anything else.

What I began to understand was that his fear of having to do one thing had driven him to offer total surrender in other areas. I also realized that what he feared was not performing sexually, for he had already done all of that, but rather the guilt and shame of someone else finding out what *he* had done. Although at nine years old, I may not have put it in exactly those words, what I now understood was that the victim's own sense of guilt and shame were tremendously powerful tools in forcing him to do more.

Having sensed this new power, I immediately fantasized a way to use it. At the time, I was regularly molesting the eight-year-old son of some friend of my parents. They lived a block away, and I had victimized that child to the point where he did not resist most demands. But I could not, despite all of my manipulations, bribes, etc., get him to perform oral sex. Nothing seemed capable of forcing him beyond his present limit. Once more, using a plan that I developed in my nightly fantasies, I told this boy that since he wasn't willing to make me happy, I was certain I could get his six-year-old brother to, especially if he knew that his big brother also played our game. A little later that afternoon, after hearing this suggestion voiced a few times, he did what I wanted. When he agreed, I felt an absolute sense of total power over him, and the twisted sensation was heightened by the fact that he was submitting to prevent two things: the shame of his brother knowing and perhaps keeping his brother from having to do it.

I was learning to use the victim's emotions as a means of gaining control over him. I was starting to play on his feelings, fears, wants, insecurities, curiosities, ego, and greed (desires) to make him do things that he didn't want to. It was also during this time that I realized that secrets were such a powerful controlling tool and began sharing secrets with potential victims as a means of proving how much I trusted them; encouraging them to prove their trust by doing the same. Ultimately, I would use the victim's absolute drive to keep his participation in these ugly acts a secret as a weapon for both keeping him silent and forcing him into even further submissions.

I was getting more proficient all the time. I now saw that certain types of boys were much more susceptible to becoming victims than others, and I began looking for boys who seemed to have particular traits. I learned what may well have been the single most important lesson in becoming a manipulative predator: I learned to listen.

By listening to a boy, sharing secrets, and encouraging him to talk about everything that was on his mind, he usually wanted to spend time with me and inadvertently provided me with all that I needed to know about his personal vulnerabilities to victimize him. I found that most people loved to talk about themselves if given the chance and that they would, once convinced you could be trusted, sit and tell you absolutely everything about both themselves and their families. I think it was clear to me even at eleven and twelve that these boys felt nobody ever really listened to them.

Before entering my teens, two additional steps were added to my escalating abusive pattern, both of which showed clear evidence of my obsession with total control. To explain the first of these additions, I have to point out something that many people don't appear to understand, or preferring to see children as totally nonsexual beings, don't want to see. All the boys I was molesting, and I, myself, were still prepubescent. None of us were yet producing semen or capable of ejaculation. But the fact that we had not yet reached puberty did not mean that we were not capable of achieving sexual climax.

If masturbated to this point, the child will go through almost the same levels of sensation that he later experiences in adulthood. Likewise, the period immediately prior to his reaching climax is one in which his body is feeling both incredible pleasure and real physical tension. When the boy does reach this nonejaculatory climax, the intensity of that moment is virtually total, and after that intense sensation, his desire for any type of sexual contact is totally ended.

These sensations were not new to me at twelve, for although I had no idea what a climax was or when it occurred, I had been masturbating for more than five years on a nightly basis. I had repeatedly seen that when a victim was close to what we called "it," (climax), it was much easier for me to get him to agree to something as a means of getting me to "make it happen." The closer that I brought him to that point, the more his body reacted, and the less likely it was for him to continue resisting. But I also had seen that once he reached "it," he was totally done for that session. All he wanted to do then was get away.

In that postclimactic state, even the most submissive of victims was finished, and no level of manipulation or pressure could get him to do anything else. I started to purposely prevent a victim from reaching climax. I would get him to submit to being masturbated, and I would bring him to a point where he was almost ready to climax and then totally stop touching him. But I only paused long enough to allow the victim to come down from the point of climaxing, without pausing long enough to allow the body tension and emotional drive to diminish. Each time that I then renewed the masturbation, the physical and emotional effects were even more acute, and his resistance was even more diminished. Seeing this reaction caused me to add new steps to my growing pattern of abuse:

9.  Control the victim's climax.
10. Tie the victim's hands and prolong climax.

I have described the twisted actions of a boy from the age

of seven to thirteen. Looking back, my abusive acts were clearly driven by my need for control and domination over something in life. I continued this escalation throughout my life and refined my abilities to manipulate and control children, but the pattern was a solid foundation and a totally accepted part of how I saw myself.

### *Amy:*

Alan continued his abuse of young boys, his victims being primarily between the ages of seven and thirteen, throughout his own teen years. His methods of manipulating them into becoming victims continued to stem from a need for control. The next series that is presented includes the actual escalations of control that Alan experienced as an adult up until the point when he was apprehended. The following pages contain sexually graphic material that the reader may find disturbing. This type of material ends with chapter nineteen and will not be revisited in the remainder of the book.

# CHAPTER SEVENTEEN

## *Alan:*
# Life as an Adult Offender

After high school I joined the military for a couple of years in the hopes I could alter my path away from pedophilia. That didn't happen. What did happen was that I met another pedophile and discovered that my horrifying acts were not just mine alone. As a clerk, I had the onerous task of completing his paperwork for a dishonorable discharge which was related to his pedophilia. Needless to say I remained silent as to our similarities and witnessed firsthand the public disgrace that accompanied our horrendous sexual perversions.

After my discharge I moved to a suburb of a large city and into a totally unfamiliar community. Not surprisingly, one of the first things I did in my efforts to get established there was to associate myself with a local church, one that, of course, sponsored a small Boy Scout troop. I went to work for a major corporation as a computer programmer and settled into a new way of life, young adulthood.

As a twenty-one-year-old, single adult in the church I quickly found myself being asked to Sunday dinner or to drinks by a variety of church families. Several of these invitations resulted in friendships, and that occupied a large portion of my weekends. I was attracted to invitations from young families who had sons, especially boys who were either in my victim age range or near it. It was clear to me that this "friend of the family" relationship held enormous potential for abusing, but it was also evident that I needed to find a new method for approaching the child. I wanted a method that would work practically in front of the parents.

Quickly my newest fantasy took shape, and the opening moves required a very new role for me. When I first began going to this type of household, I tried to act as if the boy (or children) didn't exist. I wanted to portray myself as a young man who was pleasant to children but quite clearly not overly comfortable around them. I would greet them warmly and pay a limited degree of attention to them, but I specifically worked to make people think that being around youngsters was not something I was used to or at ease with (the typical bachelor). In time, with repeated visits, and a few evenings when I might even stay in a guest room, I would let the kids grow on me, and even the parents frequently commented on how good it was to see me adjust to family life.

Though I might be willing to be talked into playing a board game or working on some type of hobby or craft, I always set a strict mental time limit for myself, and when I reached that point, I ran back for what appeared to be the need for adult company.

Slowly, I'd expand my contact with the boy I had targeted, and if my initial feelings regarding his potential were good, I would offer to let him tag along the next time I was heading out from their house to the mall or on some errand for one of his parents. Once I had the child alone, even in these brief initial instances, I fell back to the first step of the pattern that I had used for practically my entire life. I attempted to get him to "open up," and I spent a great deal of time listening.

At this point, I steered the conversation if what I heard convinced me that he was a potential victim, I continued finding ways to bring him with me and move into the testing phase.

The excitement of manipulating the boy right under his parents' noses was a new type of high for me. I frequently found myself doing things I had never considered before. On many occasions, when visiting one of my victim's homes, I would get him aside for a few moments and tell him that while I was having a drink or playing cards with his parents, he was to go to his room, remove his shirt, and take his pants down to his ankles. When he was ready, he was to call me, asking me to come see something. I would then move quickly to his room, see the boy standing exactly as I had instructed, fondle him, slip him a dollar, and return to the adults. This resulted in a tremendous feeling of being in control.

On other occasions, when there was a large house party, I'd have a boy go to one of the bathrooms and strip entirely. I would then give a particular knock, and when he let me in I would molest him. All of these were insane risks, and yet I felt I was unstoppable. Eventually, with each of these youngsters, I would be called upon to watch him on an occasion when his folks were going to be away, or I would invent a logical-sounding reason for him to stay at my house prior to our doing something "special" the next day. On that first overnight, the abuse escalated significantly.

I didn't see any of the offers of friendship that were extended to me by so many families and individuals as genuine acts of kindness, trust, and sharing. Instead I increasingly looked upon these people as using me. I mentally twisted invitations into demands—occasions when I was being asked to do something to once again keep them happy. As had always been my habit in life, I twisted reality—a distortion I then attempted to use as a mental justification for my being entitled to get what I wanted for a change. As always, I opted to see myself as the victim.

Although I had not moved to become active with the scouts, on occasion I volunteered to go on a couple of weekend overnight hikes as an adult supervisor. The elderly scoutmaster quickly realized that I was an accomplished camper and a person with a lot of scouting experience. Almost immediately, he asked me if I would be interested in joining him as an assistant. I declined.

I desperately wanted to once again be in a position where I was surrounded by young boys, but I did not want to take that step until I had the entire congregation convinced that I was doing this with extreme reluctance and only because I was practically drafted by the pastor and elders. The last thing in the world that I wanted anyone to wonder was why this single young man wanted to devote so much time to being around little boys. As I had expected, the scoutmaster discussed the matter with several of the church elders and our pastor, and I was besieged with requests to get involved.

It could not have been more than two months after joining that the old scoutmaster's health brought him to the point where he was forced to resign. The elders asked me to take over, and I declined. I made it very clear that while I had agreed to assist, I had no interest in spending one night a week "baby-sitting." I pointed out that, perhaps, when I had sons of my own that age, things would be different, but for the time being I really felt that it was more a parent's responsibility. They asked if I would at least continue to run the troop until they found a qualified replacement, and I agreed, knowing full well that they intended to use this tactic as a means of getting me to change my mind.

Now, the elders, the pastor, concerned church members, and even the parents of boys in the troop all began to contact me, asking me to reconsider. Finally, I went to the elders and told them that because I did see the need for scouting, and the need for our church to offer this important program to the boys, I would take over. However, I was worried about having to assume responsibility for all the work. I told them I could run the meetings and even find time for the camp outs, but if I also had to do all of the administrative work, fund-raising, etc., I wouldn't have time for a personal life. I offered to do my share but only if the church would support my efforts.

At this point, everyone in the church knew that I did not want the job that was all but being forced on me. But no one else wanted it either, especially none of the fathers of the boys in the troop. Committees were set up to handle transportation, administration, testing, finance, and so on. I made it very clear that I'd accepted only because I saw they wanted me to do the job and because of all the support they were willing to offer.

The image I needed was now in place. Should anyone raise the question as to why this new young man spent so much time with these kids, the entire neighborhood and congregation would explain just how hard they had to work to talk me into it.

One of the first things I did when taking over the troop was to talk my friends with scout-age sons (most of whom were currently victims to one degree or another) into enrolling those boys in the troop. In doing so, I immediately had new, approved reasons for having access to them overnight. Although I was on old familiar ground once again, I discovered that being an adult required that I make certain modifications to my method of approaching boys.

While I was still only about twenty-two, my adult status initially seemed to be a major stumbling block to most of the boys feeling comfortable in opening up to me. It was apparent to me that from now on the primary aim in my first few steps with each victim would be to give him a sense that I was really much closer to him than I was to the adult world. It did not take long to develop a series of lines that communicated this to most kids, and they began to see me as being different from other adults. I began the standard routine of listening, sharing secrets, and escalation.

The first few encounters in my approach were now a bit different, but I also learned that having adult status, transportation, my own place to take victims, and the financial means to offer significantly improved bribes proved to more than offset any initial resistance that I encountered. Most of the potential victims were awed to suddenly be receiving special attention from their new, young scoutmaster, and within a month or two, I was taking the first sexual step with a new victim.

It was also during this time period that I became the camp master of a six-acre scout camp on the outskirts of the city. This was a tiny wooded area that was frequently used by local troops for easy weekend camping and one in desperate need of repair and maintenance. I volunteered to bring a few boys out each weekend to work, and as a result, I was given a small cabin in the middle of the property to use when I wanted to stay over.

This camp and private cabin provided a perfect stop to take

victims, in addition to my apartment. The fact that it was located only ten or fifteen minutes from town made it even more attractive to me. By taking youngsters there for a weekend of community service as a cover and having a private cabin available, I quickly got involved with a larger number of boys.

By the age of twenty-four, I had established a comfortable niche for myself and was reasonably accustomed to my new lifestyle. Looking back, perhaps the most striking thing I recall being conscious of at that time was that there really wasn't going to be a future, at least not one in "their" sense of the word. It wasn't a foreboding sense of doom or disaster, just the realization that, for me, nothing ever truly would change. It was clear to me that the physical aspects of my environment had changed, but my private mental world was totally unaltered. There had been times in the past, albeit not many of them, when I had some small hope that all of my thoughts and actions might yet be something that I would eventually outgrow. Now, even that faint, infrequent idea seemed foolish to me. Whenever I heard friends or business associates speak in terms of where they hoped to be in five or ten years, it seemed alien to me.

There was, of course, no way that I could see myself as having responsibility for any of this. To my mind, I was the victim. How could a person be responsible for something over which he had no control? After all, I had not wanted to be a pedophile. It was a matter over which I was never given a choice. I was, according to my view, different—born, defective, broken—and that state of being different was absolute and unalterable. Pedophilia was something I was forced to live with.

In the period since my arrest, I have often been asked if I hated or loved my victims and/or their parents. And the answer is probably both. Some of "them" I liked and enjoyed more than other "thems." But "they" were never "me," and my liking or disliking "them" would never really play a role in what I did. My sense of detachment was so complete that I never viewed what I did as being, in any sense personal.

If I stopped at a "friend's" home, spent time, had dinner and a few drinks, and then took his son home and molested him, I saw no betrayal or anything personal in any of it. By working to constantly maintain my feeling of victimization along with a sense of total detachment from every other person, I could view people as things and blame them for my point of view.

By my early twenties, I saw a twisted type of balance in life. We clearly lived jointly, in two different worlds. In their world, I was a monster, a thing. And in my world they, while not being monsters, were very much things. As a self-created victim, I chose to see "them" as always using me, therefore I felt no qualms about my using "them."

In this mindset, I would have no more qualms about using your child than I would of using your car. My view was clear. In their world, they controlled me, and in my world, I controlled everything.

By twenty-four, I had two different means of accessing potential victims: through friendship with their parents or through the scout troop. I employed a method and pattern of abuse I'd been creating and refining for seventeen years, and I had no fear that my victims would ever inform on me. The tools at my disposal as an adult were a great deal more powerful than those I had in earlier years, and as a result, I was molesting on a scale that even I would not have thought possible five years earlier. Now I had a constant pool of young victims in various degrees of molestation, a pool that had to contain somewhere in the neighborhood of forty to fifty youngsters. I distinctly remember attending a church Christmas pageant at this time, and of the eleven boys on the stage, nine of them were current victims.

From experience, I knew that the usual result of a victim's arriving at puberty was an increased desperation on his part to find a workable way to end his abuse. If his abuse started at nine or ten, by thirteen of fourteen, he had been abused so frequently, and in his mind had allowed it to continue for so long, that he felt totally incapable of telling anyone about any of it. He was held a silent prisoner to his own misguided sense of guilt and shame. Although the eleven- or twelve-year-old was totally disgusted by what he was being forced to endure, he would almost always rather submit than ever risk the mortal shame of anyone's finding out.

As these victims approached puberty, however, the growing sense of adolescent independence was making further submission more and more intolerable. By thirteen, the average victim of my abuse was searching desperately for some way to end it but to do so without having to make any of it known to anyone. In earlier years, when it took me significantly longer to totally escalate a victim, this adolescent sense of independence occurred at just about the same time that I was losing interest in the boy.

During my early twenties, however, armed with an array of new and more powerful tools, the time it took me to escalate a victim was reduced. In a short time, I was finding that the ten- and eleven-year-old victims who surrounded me were already at the point of mental resignation long before the onset of puberty and adolescent independence.

I had spent the previous two years grooming, bribing, and molesting these boys and getting them accustomed to receiving enormous amounts of time, attention, and rewards. I had also worked to instill a twisted understanding of friendship in each of them and particularly to make each one feel special. They were not yet at the point where they realized that they didn't need this perverted type of attention, and when I attempted to withdraw from them, most reacted from a sense of being suddenly rejected.

In essence, while they had reached the point of submission where I no longer found any thrill in controlling and abusing them, they had not reached the point where they would silently drift away. To further compound an already complex situation, being an adult also meant that I was in a position where I could not just disappear. In childhood, it is not at all uncommon for boys to have close friends who they then drift away from. Parents are used to seeing childhood friendships come and go, and while there might be a few general questions, they accept it as a normal phase of social development.

Many of my current victims, on the other hand, were the sons of people with whom I was very friendly. In several instances, I spent time at the homes of these boys and their families, and for me to abruptly discontinue an established pattern could cause serious questions. Even in those cases where the child was not the son of a close acquaintance, he was still a member of the scout troop. And not only did I not want to give up being scoutmaster, but doing so suddenly would lead to publicity, questions, and potential problems.

In short, for the first time in my life, I found myself surrounded by a host of young victims who no longer offered me what I was looking for but whom I had no safe way of cutting off. I had to continue maintaining the same relative level of attention, time, and rewards that I had made them accustomed to. I point out again that none of these youngsters wanted me to continue any type of abuse with them, but all of them were still young enough to want the attention and special treatment that I had been providing them in other areas. Having to do this was something I, as always, turned into something I viewed as my being victimized. They no longer resisted, they gave me practically everything I wanted, except for the thrill that I wanted most.

For me, there was no excitement and certainly no sense of control; if anything, I felt that they were controlling me. As I could see no way of safely discontinuing my associations with these victims, it was clear to me that I needed to find some way to make them more exciting for me. Excitement came with the feeling of control, and control meant making them do something beyond what I had demanded in the past. What I needed now was to do something that excited me, something that I knew they would be extremely unwilling to do and then force them once again into submission.

I began spending nights fantasizing about different ideas, attempting to find something that caught my imagination, and to heighten these fantasy sessions, I turned, as was now my habit, to the fuel of child pornography. Before long, the next escalation came into focus. I refined my fantasy into a workable plan, targeted a specific initial victim. I went out and purchased my first instant camera.

Typically, I picked the most vulnerable of this entire vulnerable collection of victims. He was a youngster with a difficult home life and one who for the most part was almost entirely ignored by the mother and grandparents raising him. He was one of the youngsters who had called me repeatedly, asking to be taken for the weekend, and who seemed to have the attitude that being sexually abused and getting a little something out of it was better than staying home, being abused in a different fashion, and getting nothing.

Anytime that I have a tendency to slip back into my old victim mentality I bring this child to mind, and the horror of what I put him through quickly puts into focus who the victim of my crimes really is. At this stage, however, he was just another thing and the thing that I had picked to try out this exciting new type of abuse.

I stopped by his house during the week and got permission to take him to camp over the weekend. I picked him up on Friday night, and we headed directly to my cabin. I then told him that he had two choices. First, we could just hang around the camp for the weekend and do what we normally did, spending the days doing maintenance chores and letting him drive the Jeep, or if he was willing, we could try something a bit more fun. We would do something for him tomorrow that I knew he loved, and I'd see to it that he would have a fantastic time.

His part of the deal was to be willing to try something new tomorrow night, and I quickly pointed out that this new thing did not involve any physical act he hadn't already done nor did it involve anyone but the boy and myself. I flatly refused to provide any details, wanting to keep his sense of anticipation high, and said that it was just a blind agreement. If he said yes, we did it, and if he said no, we'd stick to hanging around camp.

I guess he figured that if we were alone and he had done it before, he could suffer through it again, so he agreed. Early the next day, I got him up, took him out to breakfast, and then surprised him by taking him to the local amusement park. For the rest of the day, he was allowed to go on whatever rides he wanted and was plied with snacks and soda. And throughout the day, I would periodically remind him that I expected his cooperation when we got home. He didn't seem surprised when instead of driving back to camp, I took him to my house, but when I took him into my bedroom and he saw the camera and several boxes of film, he went white.

It was instantly clear that the idea of being photographed terrified him. Like all of my victims, this boy lived in constant fear that someone might suspect what he was doing, and the idea of putting it on film had him almost in tears. The minute I saw the extent of his reluctance, the old electric thrill was surging, and the game was back in play.

On that first night, I did manage to photograph him, but not nearly to the degree I had intended. By playing on his sense of obligation for his day at the park, I got him to submit to eight photos (one box of film). The first showed him fully clothed, and each successive picture showed him with one fewer article of clothing … but only down to his undershorts. I remember that I tried to get the final, naked photo, but the best I could do on that first attempt was to allow the eighth shot to clearly show that beneath the fabric of his shorts, he was erected. His resistance had been even greater than I had fantasized, and although he did submit to these eight pictures, he only did so if I avoided including his face in any shot. I went along with what he wanted, and even this series of photographs was exciting for me.

Once again I was watching a victim do something he dreaded and had real trouble dealing with. What followed was a surprisingly slow escalation. In time, the same boy submitted to being photographed nude but still without his face in any picture. With more manipulations and bribes, he ultimately surrendered and allowed himself to be filmed in a variety of naked poses, including pictures of him masturbating. Each photo showed all of him, including his full face. I then expanded the collection to include him in different settings, some of which were done outdoors, and finally to a series that showed him bound and gagged in simulated sadistic acts. Eventually even that thrill was wearing thin, so I began with the next boy.

With each successive victim, regardless of the number and variety of photos I ended up taking, I took one eight-shot series in which I posed each boy naked in perfectly identical poses in the same setting. When I had completed this series with the second victim, I laid both the boy's shots out next to each other and was captivated by a sense of power in being able to demand identical performances from each of them. In time, the number of victims in those photos as well as my sense of control grew tremendously.

Before long, there were twenty-two medium-sized brown envelopes locked in a wooden chest in my bedroom. Each envelope contained an entire photographic record of a different victim. All of my photographed victims had now reached the point where they were no longer resisting being filmed. The most exciting part at this point was laying out one identically posed shot for each of the boys and experiencing a surge of power knowing that I had forced all of them to do exactly the same thing in exactly the same place despite their fear of being recorded.

On many occasions, I would then shuffle those snapshots like a deck of playing cards and randomly deal myself a victim for the coming weekend. As I would sit and stare at the photos of these different victims, there was a twisted delight in knowing that I could just pick one and do practically anything to him. I knew that any conceivable sexual perversion was readily obtainable, but there was no further excitement, no challenge, and especially none of the thrill that came with watching a victim reach the difficult moment of surrender.

## Outline of a Large-Scale Obsessive Offense

There are several elements involved with my obsessive offenses for control that I feel are particularly important to gaining an insight into what drives them.

1. The original idea was usually something that was not overly difficult for me to either plan out or implement.
2. Some unique part of the idea captivated me, and instead of fantasizing a plan to act out, I remained in the fantasy mode and continually escalated the level of the intended abuse.
3. I began to do things that were unnecessary in order to obtain my goal, i.e. making endless lists, notes, and forms, in order to both heighten the excitement and prolong the fantasy.
4. As long as I remained in the fantasy mode, I continued to expand the level of abuse and ultimately reached the point where due to my investment of time, energy, and money in the plan, I visualized myself as the victim and used this distortion for even further escalation.
5. I became more and more obsessed with the fantasy until I reached the point, normally in the week prior to acting out, where virtually everything else in my life meant nothing to me, and I concentrated on nothing else.
6. I continually played one victim against the other, maintaining control by means of additional bribes, and secrets, always endeavoring to have each victim believe that he was not the object of the abuse, but rather more of a contributing bystander.

7. I went to inordinate lengths in providing bribes and inducements, as well as in elaborately staging the final acting out.

8. I was completely obsessed with the ritualistic nature of the actual abuse. Crucial to me was the slow and deliberate pace, the continual escalation of each phase, and especially the adamant demand that each victim play out his role precisely as I intended it.

I have attempted to depict this series of incidents, not as I see them today, but rather as I chose to see and feel them at the time that they took place. In doing this, I have purposely included words that are grossly inappropriate when describing the abuse of an innocent victim. When I use terms such as "happy," "delighted," "willing," "eager," they are not intended to portray the victim's actual mental state, for clearly none of them apply. They are used solely to let you see the world as I wanted to believe it at that time.

I would like to clarify my use of the word "ritual" in regard to the acting out of my obsessive fantasies. I saw these abuses as rituals because by the time that I actually acted them out, I had pictured them so vividly and so frequently in my imagination that their ultimate enactment had a distinctly ritualistic feeling for me. I also refer to these occasions as rituals because their implementation was intentionally prolonged by my forcing my victim(s) to submit to a series of escalating steps, all of which were totally unnecessary to obtaining my sexual goal.

It should also be rather obvious that even the most unsophisticated of my young victims could often "see through" what I was leading them into. What I would ask you to keep in mind is that by the time a victim reached this stage of awareness, he was usually already emotionally defeated to the degree that he viewed his continued abuse as virtually inevitable and saw this crude technique as just another part of this insane game. I spent a great deal of time trying to get victims to disassociate themselves, to mentally dull the reality and pretend that all of the horror wasn't real.

On many occasions, however, such as the one that I am about to relate, the victim, while seeing through the immediate manipulation, remained unaware until the final moment that there was an additional step involved, something for which they were totally unprepared.

What follows is an example of the extreme, but it contains elements within this highly obsessed behavior, and these elements are fundamentals that just about every pedophile employs to one degree or another.

Tragically, the incident is true, and even my best attempt to portray it fails to convey the mental and emotional impact it had on my young victims. To fulfill my obsession, I worked to bring these victims to the point of demonstrating that there was virtually nothing that I could not get them to do. And in doing this, I destroyed whatever shreds of self-respect that remained following two years of abuse. Don't look at this incident strictly in terms of the physical perversions, for as disgusting as they are, it is not the physical but the mental and emotional devastation that ultimately causes the greatest damage to these boys.

In the winter of my twenty-fourth year, even the new excitement of photographing victims was failing to produce the thrills I wanted. Although I still looked forward to filming new victims, as what was now a standard part of my abusive pattern, I knew that I wanted to escalate, and I knew the direction that I wanted my escalation to take. I had begun bringing together two victims on a limited basis, and now I wanted to expand that form of abuse.

In my teens, I had primarily used an older victim to help me get a new victim to take his first major step toward abuse. What this usually amounted to was bringing the victims and myself together, and having my previous victim suggest, during the course of the night, that we play cards, leading to his then suggesting we make it into a dare type game. The result of these first attempts had been that the new victim ended up reaching the point of exposing himself, and following this initial step, I would escalate his abuse without involving the other boy. Earlier I had escalated my pattern by forcing the older victim to actually continue through the next few steps of the younger boy's sexual abuse. I had reached the point of watching them as they were forced to perform orally on each other. In all of my earlier cases, however, the younger victim, having had the other boy present from the very onset of his abuse, did not see his presence as anything out of the ordinary for these sessions.

I planned to bring together two victims who had both been repeatedly molested by me over a period of more than two years, but neither of whom had ever been abused in the presence of anyone but me. To compound the situation, both of these victims had been carefully groomed to believe that they were the only friend of mine special enough to be trusted to play my game.

Even when I initially thought about bringing two current victims together for joint abuse, it was clear to me that it would be relatively easy to arrange what I had in mind. There were some difficulties, but certainly nothing that I could not talk and bribe my way around, and I was certain that by taking two of the most submissive of my victims with me on a weekend camping trip, plying them with liquor, and offering a few increased bribes, I could then suggest that we play cards and quickly escalate the game to practically any level I wanted. In fact, this very idea was to turn into a total obsession.

I knew that the two victims I would end up taking had to be among the most submissive and completely abused of the boys I was involved with, and I realized that I had a complete photo record of every boy who fit into that category. At night, I laid out one identically posed photograph of each of these boys and then arranged the pictures into possible pairs. In doing this, I had a tremendous sense of power; knowing that, without any of them being aware of it, I could combine them in any way that I wished and make that combination a reality. Enjoying that sense of control, I laid these photos out every night, sorting and resorting them, and feeling incredibly powerful.

I don't think that there was ever any real doubt in my mind as to who the first two victims were to be, but the nightly process was nonetheless exciting to me. I didn't want to make the final selection until I had milked this process for all that it was worth. To heighten my sense of power, I designed a fact sheet to add to each boy's photographic file. It took me several days until I had a satisfactory form, and the final product contained the following types of information:

1. Personal data
   Full name
   Age/Date of birth
   Height
   Weight

Color of hair

Color of eyes

A variety of physical measurements (all of which were taken and recorded when I began using the form).

2. History (of abuse)

Length of time involved

List of every sexual perversion (in a coded abbreviation) that would be checked if the boy had performed it, and if checked, followed by a rating (from 1 to 5).

3. Family information

Here I listed all family information that either helped or hindered my access to the child. And once again rated, on a 1 to 5 scale, what I viewed as my ease of access to him for overnight and weekend exploitation.

4. Unique data

Hobbies

Likes and dislikes

Names of closest friends

Names of youngsters he had previous problems with

Medical problems

Tolerance for liquor

Tolerance for tranquilizers

Any other data that might affect pairing him with others.

I need to point out at this juncture that *none* of this was *in any way necessary*. With the exception of the detailed personal measurements, I knew every fact on these sheets by heart for every victim. That had nothing to do with the fact that completing this form for each of these boys heightened my sense of power, and prolonged the thrill that the process gave me.

During this period of recording and mental pairing, I met

with the boys in the troop, two at a time, under the pretense of discussing advancement and future troop activities. At our weekly meetings, I would bring together pairs of randomly selected boys and speak with them at a small table I had set up in a room that adjoined our usual meeting room. I distinctly remember the first time that I sat there with two possible joint victims sitting together, neither having the slightest idea that the boy next to him, if I wanted, would end up being his sexual partner. I felt totally electric—absolutely dominant.

# CHAPTER EIGHTEEN

## *Alan:*
# Escalation

### The First Escalation

Despite all of the extra steps that I'd added to the selection process, my plan up until this point had always been to pick two victims, take them together for a weekend, and force them to perform jointly. While the idea that I could pick any two and make this happen was exciting to me, I now began thinking of something even more exciting—something which would prove that I had even more control over both victims.

I became fascinated with the element of the unknown and decided that if bringing victims face to face and forcing them to perform was exciting and controlling, then getting each of them to agree to performing sexually with an unknown partner, prior to taking them for the weekend, would be even more so.

The idea of having both boys know ahead of time that on a specific night they would be introduced to someone and forced to have sex, but not knowing who that person was ahead of time, utterly captivated my imagination. My obsession now moved to a higher level.

Once this new concept struck me, I decided to get serious and make the actual selection. And despite the prolonged process, I selected exactly the same two youngsters whom I'd initially thought about.

Adam was the boy who had been my first photographic victim. He had been abused frequently and allowed my ejaculation during oral sex. He offered no resistance to my demands. And, as previously mentioned, I had almost total access to him. He had just turned thirteen but had not yet entered puberty.

Paul was twelve and the son of some friends I'd gotten close to through the church. His family and I had spent weekends together, and Paul and I had also gone camping. I had almost limitless access to him. He had been my victim for a little more than two years. During the previous summer, I had taken Paul and his younger brother camping for a week while his parents were off somewhere. Both he and his brother were included in my photographic files, but neither knew that the other was involved. I had toyed with the idea of making these two brothers my first joint victims but had stayed away from that fearing possible sibling rivalry or some other conflict that I could not control.

Knowing that both Paul and Adam were totally groomed, totally submissive victims, I realized getting them to have sex with an unknown partner was easily accomplishable. Both might initially resist the idea, but I was convinced that, with the right type of bribes, both could be brought to the point of agreeing.

Since both victims were at the mental state of viewing their abuse as something that they were incapable of avoiding, my selecting the right bribe for each of them would usually make their surrendering to what they saw as inevitable a much quicker process. Both kids were fishing and camping fanatics. I immediately decided that a special type of fishing weekend, something that they could share, would more than likely bring them to the point I wanted.

In my fantasies, I figured out different ways of staging their initial meeting. I was looking for a way that would be the most exciting for me to both put together and observe. I was fascinated by imagining what they would look like and how each of them would react at the instant that they discovered whom their intended partner was to be. And it was during these imaginings that I once again escalated the level of my obsession.

## The Second Escalation

I was obsessed with the concept of keeping the two victims dangling in a state of mental suspense, a state of escalating anxiety, doubt, and trepidation. Both would know exactly what they would be made to do and when they would be forced to do it, but until immediately before it happened, neither would know who the other was.

The thrill in all this was the mysterious element of the unknown. It was producing an incredible sense of control for me. During the course of running dozens of different ideas about how to finally bring them together, I realized that there was a way for me to prove an even greater level of control over these victims. If getting them to agree to have sex together before they knew each other's identity demonstrated my power and control, then how much greater control would be shown if I could make them actually perform with each other without first knowing the identity of the other body involved? When I thought of this, I was instantly obsessed, totally electric, and although I had no idea how or where I was going to make all of this into a reality, there wasn't the slightest doubt in my mind that I would be able to do so.

In a recent copy of the state's Department of Environmental Conservation magazine, I read an article about the opening of a new wilderness area in the nearby mountains. As it was late enough in the spring that the weather would permit easy camping, I headed up there on a three-day weekend to check the place out. It proved to be a totally isolated spot, with camping on two small islands—total, inaccessible privacy. I shot several rolls of 35-millimeter film, taking care to show the beauty of the location.

I recalled that a park ranger informed me that the number of campers being allowed in for the initial season would be strictly limited and that it would be wise for me to purchase a permit in advance. This I did, receiving a permit for three weeks in late July and early August. The form required my listing the names of the "people in my party," and I listed myself, Adam and Paul. I had yet to talk to either boy, nor had I even hinted to the parents about taking either child for an extended summer outing, but it never crossed my mind that anything could possibly stand in my way.

I was growing more and more obsessed with my fantasy. Upon my return home, I immediately got this three-week period approved as vacation time and had the rolls of film developed. Next I visited with both sets of parents and shared with them the photos of this beautiful park. I let each of them know that I was planning to return to this wilderness for two or three weeks during the summer, and that if possible, I would take a few of the scouts with me.

My selling point to them was that with only eight or nine campsites open, this virgin forest afforded the boys an opportunity to experience an area untouched by civilization—something unusual these days. By the following year, I pointed out, the number of sites would be dramatically increased, and while the natural beauty would still remain, the thrill of being among the first allowed to explore the area would be gone.

The parents agreed to let me take their sons, and I explained that until I had worked out the final details, I'd prefer the children not know of our plans. I told them that while I was positive I would be going, I still wasn't sure for how long. Until I had it arranged, I didn't want to excite the kids only to disappoint them.

Both boys had seen the photos of the campsite, and both waited until we were alone before asking if I would be going back there and if I would take them. I let each boy know that this was exactly what I had in mind.

Each was told that I wanted to take my special friend for two weeks, but they were not to say anything to their parents about any of this until I had a chance to speak with them and get them to agree to the plan. During both of these conversations, I made it quite clear that I was looking forward to being free to play my games at night, and both youngsters, caught up in the excitement of a prolonged fishing and camping trip, assured me that I could do anything I wanted.

Two months before the trip I was not fantasizing about anything but what I intended for these two victims. I'd told each of them they would be going for a two-week outing, leaving myself the third week as an additional manipulative tool. I needed to fantasize a plan to implement what I wanted, and I broke the entire process down into progressive phases and started working out the details.

In the past, I had always found that one of the most effective ways to manipulate a victim was to get him to expect a certain thing and then at the last moment inform him that a problem had arisen, which through no fault of my own, prevented my delivering all of what I had originally intended. Following this shock, I would present the victim with a fictitious problem (the obvious solution to which was always his agreeing to some greater level of abuse), and I asked him to help me figure out a solution. As his initial desire had already been heightened and built on and as he was already in a state where he viewed continued abuse as unavoidable, it only took fast talking and a few increased bribes to bring him to where he would offer up exactly what I wanted from him. This basic tactic was precisely what I had in mind for these boys.

Some people have asked me how I went about figuring out all the manipulations that I employed over the years, and my answer was "I didn't have to figure them out.... They were always right there for me."

When you have spent your entire life hiding, distorting, and manipulating, you don't really have to sit down and think about it too much. True, I used my fantasies to work out details, but even in doing that, I was using this method more for the nightly high it provided me than for any real necessity in planning. My fantasies would allow me to refine and script what I had in mind, but manipulating was a way of life for me, and every time I encountered a situation, my first instinct was to address it with manipulation.

That being the case, I knew immediately that I intended to execute a four-stage scenario prior to the final act. In implementing the plan, each boy was provided with the identical setup and story.

## STAGE I

This stage had already taken place. The potential victim was offered a prize, and over the next several weeks, I worked to heighten his desire for it and his expectation of it.

## STAGE II

After two or three weeks of building the anticipation for the proposed two-week trip, I told each boy that a problem had come up, and that unless I, or we, could figure out a solution, I would be forced to make it a one-week trip instead.

The problem I explained was that I'd promised to watch a friend's son for one week during the summer, and it turned out to be one of the weeks we were planning to be away. I took care to explain that we could not just take him along, even though he was a great kid, because doing that would mean that I could not indulge in my nightly fun.

I admitted to each of the boys that it was a really stupid situation, but because I trusted him, I would share the real problem with him, hoping that he might see a way to solve it that I had overlooked. I then told each of them that this other boy was someone whom I'd known even before I had met him.

I assured him that the other boy was a fantastic kid, and that I had gone on several trips during the summer with his family. On those trips, I explained, in order to save his family some money, I agreed to share my motel room with the youngster. And, in doing that we too had "played" around. I then made it clear that this other boy had played the same kind of games we had, and that because he was familiar with my kind of fun, there was no way to bring him along without his knowing what we were doing at night when he wasn't looking.

I added that I really didn't care about his knowing that we were doing it because I trusted him totally, but I wouldn't

want either of my two closest friends to be put into an embarrassing situation. I concluded by saying that the only way I
could see to work things out, without embarrassing either
friend, was to take one boy for the first week, then drive him
home, and take the second one back for the second week.

Then I added the fantasized setup. I pointed out that it
was a rotten solution because by doing that, both boys lost
out on a week's fishing, and I had double the expense in driving back and forth to the mountains. And, I added, all of this
loss of time and extra expense was just to keep two great kids
from seeing together what they both would see separately
anyway. I then asked each of them to think about it and see if
they had any ideas. I'd talk to them during our next scout
meeting.

The first question that each boy asked was, of course,
"who is the other boy," but I explained that it really wouldn't
be fair of me to name him, and that as a good friend, I would
never tell on someone. In order to make each of them feel
special, I pointed out that he was the only person I had discussed the problem with, the other kid had no idea that he
even existed.

## STAGE III

During the next scout meeting. I met with each victim separately. Adam immediately suggested our all going together,
and Paul, while not making this offer at the outset, did so
when it was clear to him that without a solution, I was cutting his trip to one week.

At this point each of them was told the following:

> "You're a fantastic kid, my closest friend, and I knew I
> could really count on you to help figure this out. I'd
> been thinking the same thing, but I hadn't suggested it

because I didn't want you to feel I was forcing it on you. After all, I would never do anything to embarrass you."

I explained that we still didn't know if it would work because I'd have to explain it all to the other boy, and he still might be too embarrassed to go along with "our" plan. Following which I slipped each boy a couple of dollars as a token of how much I appreciated his going out of his way to help me out.

## STAGE IV

The following day I invented a reason to speak with each boy and once again presented them with identical stories.

The other boy was not real sure, but that I had talked him into going along. But he'd insisted that it would be better if we got together and played around before the trip. If that worked out well, then he'd know the trip would be easy. But if it didn't work, then he could still change his mind and go for one week alone.

I had tried to assure the other boy that things would be fine, but he tended to be shy and insisted on a test before we left.

When I saw that I couldn't change his mind, it dawned on me that at least we might use this test as a means of letting him help me persuade the other boy and by doing that pick up a few interesting prizes.

I then explained that this other boy did everything but was shy about doing it with someone else there. But if the victim I was talking to could go through the "test" with him, and let him see how easy it was, then the other kid would feel totally relaxed and be dying to go. Now I explained that in order to make all of this as easy as possible for the other kid, I had suggested that the three of us turn a night at the local camp into a type of game show. I would invent a series of really crazy contests, all of which were intended to get the other kid to relax, and that in addition to just seeing that all of this would work out, I would come up with prizes for each of them for every event.

At that point, I tossed out the first of two setup lines. I made it clear that he really didn't need this test, and I knew he was only going along to help me solve the problem and get all of us to end up having two weeks together. And I really appreciated his efforts. Because I knew he didn't need this kind of test, but was still willing to go through it, I wanted to do something special for him, and what I had decided was to give him what he was saving me.

I pointed out that if the other kid insisted on his own week, it was going to cost me an additional twenty dollars in gas and snacks, driving back and forth. But if this victim was willing to go through the game show test, and go out of his way to make it all look both fun and easy for the other kid, I'd let him have the twenty bucks as spending money for the trip. But of course, as much as I liked the other kid, I didn't want him to find out about this bonus, or he would feel cheated.

Both victims agreed immediately, and I reminded them that in order to put the other kid totally at ease, I was really going to create a "nutty" night, one that would let us do what "we" had in mind, but do it in such a strange way, the kid would feel more comfortable. Some of it might seem a bit kidlike to him and a little on the unnecessary side, but that's why he was getting paid a bonus.... to go along with everything without any problems or questions and in doing so, help to get the other kid to do the same. Again, both told me to relax, that they could make this kid feel at home, and the game show approach would be fine with them.

Both asked what kind of extra prizes I was thinking about. My final comment was that the prizes would depend on how tough I made the events, and I thought I'd leave that "up to him." If he wanted really great prizes, I could dream up some really far-out stunts, if not ... I'd come up with lesser ideas. Both boys told me to make them as hard as I could.

With the completion of these four stages, I had accomplished the original intent of my fantasy. Both victims had agreed to perform sexually with someone, without knowing who the other person was. The fantasy had long since become an obsession, and despite the two escalations that had already taken place, my obsession was still growing. I arranged to close the local campground on the following weekend by informing the staff at the scout council that I needed the camp shut down to do some maintenance. I also arranged with their parents that the two boys come with me to do a service project at the camp. My feeling of control was skyrocketing, and as the actual date was drawing near, I was finding it virtually impossible to concentrate on anything but that Friday night.

I'd already reached the point where I had designed the test, and now my fantasies, both night and day, were centered on getting every aspect of what I had in mind down to precise detail. By this point, my obsession with the idea was almost total, and when it reached that point, there is practically nothing I wouldn't do to make it into a reality. I had spent a tremendous amount of time setting things up, and now I fully intended to get the absolute maximum in return.

All I could picture in my mind was putting the two of them through a mental and physical maze of my design. I concentrated on the overall staging of three tests I'd thought up and planned them in precise detail. I also figured out just what prizes would most easily get my victims to overcome their reservations.

Money was to be the prize for the first test, and a variety of fishing lures and line were to be the prize for the second. It was when I was designing the tests, thinking about the fact that my current obsession would take three weeks of my time and cost several hundred dollars to execute, that I had decided on how to use the still unannounced third week of camping. As I looked at the time, effort, money, and energy that I was pouring into my plan, I didn't want to see it as being of my own doing. So, typically for my distorted thinking, I began to see me as being victimized by "them."

To my twisted thinking, I was going through all of it to give them three weeks summer vacation. Worse, all they were offering in return was slightly more than what they had been giving all along. As I mulled it all over, I convinced myself that for what I was being put through, I was clearly entitled to demand more from both of them. It was then that my obsession took its final escalation. I would offer the third week but only for a very different price.

One of the reasons I recall the prizes so clearly is that the obsessive lengths I went to stage this entire abuse found me going to the local sporting goods store and picking up brochures with photos of all the items I would be offering. My plan was to provide the victims with all of this merchandise but to have it with me when we left on the trip, rather than risk having them show up at home ahead of time with a bunch of new things. The cash was no problem, for I would see to it that both of them spent it during the trip. Likewise, the assorted fishing tackle would all be "used" and tossed into their tackle boxes by the time we returned.

For the ultimate prize, I decided to offer each of them a

fishing pole and spring reel, and although I could not cover this up as easily, I planned for making it seem perfectly understandable. Each boy, if they won their pole, would be told to bring his oldest, most beat-up pole on the trip. Then, I would have them discard these, explaining to their parents that they were lost overboard, forcing me to pick up a new one ... no big deal. Under those circumstances, it was highly unlikely that the parent would question me.

I cut pictures from the brochures and pasted them onto cardboard sheets. This gave something of the look of the prizes shown on TV game shows. I made one set for each victim. The rest of that week was spent making detailed lists of what I would need to have with me, what I would require in each of the three tests, and even sketches of the rooms in the old wooden building at the camp where I intended to act all of this out.

Each day my obsession grew, and by Wednesday, anything not directly related to the execution of the fantasy was out of the question. I'd been collecting all the items I planned on using, getting the food and drinks that we would need, and most of all, going over every individual step of the entire abuse again and again.

On Wednesday night, I loaded most of the collected materials into my car. At midday on Thursday, I drove over to the camp to see that everything was going to be closed as I wanted it. When I was assured that such was the case, I went to the building to make certain that the items I needed were there and in place. Thursday night I stopped by the victims' houses to give them each a pep talk. I reemphasized the fact that "he" was the one I was counting on to pull this off as "we" had planned it, not failing to remind each about the bonus payment for his setting an example.

I let them know that I had spent a lot of time trying to come up with some way that would make all of this a bit more fun for each of them. I assured them that the prizes were good ones, and the only thing I was concerned about was that both of them would work well together, so that they could both end up with a two-week trip. Each boy assured me that he would see to it that the other went along with our plan.

# CHAPTER NINETEEN

## *Alan:*
# The Ritual

I had designed the three tests to make the process as demanding of both victims as possible. In putting all of this together, I spent countless hours thinking about what would be the hardest things for both of these youngsters to handle. In the end, it had come down to three different levels of abuse. First, to admit to the other victim everything they'd ever submitted to (something which I knew that both dreaded); second, to perform those same acts with this still-unknown partner; and finally, to be forced to go beyond anything that he had expected.

The process was sexual, and extremely sadistic, although not in the physical way. What I wanted (and was determined to get) was to have both youngsters see the other, and then himself, totally give up. I wanted both to feel that they were powerless to resist anything.

The key element in this fantasy had always been the unknown, and I wanted to keep that element in place until the very end. In order to arrange this, I had asked Paul's dad to drop him off at the camp at a specific time that night, leaving me free to pick up Adam, arrive before they did, and get the first victim prepared for what was about to take place. When everything at the camp was set up, I left to get the first victim.

I don't want to go into exact detail regarding what I subjected these boys to, nor do I think that it's necessary. But to provide you with a feeling for my now-insane obsession with controlling every minute detail about what took place, I will roughly touch on the procedure and then give an outline of each test. However, I would once again remind you that the sexual outcome was never in doubt. Even the final, hardest demand I believed was a virtual certainty. Therefore, everything that occurred served no purpose other than to prove my domination.

When I brought Adam into the building, the first thing I did was to give him a cold soda laced with a very large amount of vodka. He was accustomed to having liquor as a prelude to abuse and quickly ingested the drink. Next I explained that although I knew he didn't need testing, I wanted him to go through exactly the same steps as the other kid to make it look real and to put the other boy at ease. He said he had no problem with this, and I then explained that in order to make it a bit more interesting, I designed a game that would keep both of them in the dark about who the other was until later that night.

I handed him a blindfold I'd put together, with an elastic back to keep it snugly in place. He tried it on, and I tested it to make sure he could not see. I told him that when the other boy arrived, I would have to get him ready also. During that time, Adam would wait in one of the small rooms. Finally I told him that the key to making all of this work was that neither of them was to say a word.

I would give instructions, and they would carry them out without any talking. He agreed, and we sat having a smoke until about five minutes prior to Paul's scheduled arrival. I then took the boy into one of the small rooms, which I had equipped with a chair, and told him that he was to remain there until I had the other kid ready.

When Paul arrived, I met him in the parking lot and talked with his father for a few minutes. After his dad left, I gave him the same instructions I'd given Adam. I told him that once we entered the building, there could be no speaking. He agreed. I took him inside, gave him the same type of drink, and took him into the big meeting room, which I had set up for the actual abuse. I'd taken one end of this large room and divided it into two separate sections by hanging a canvas tarp from the ceiling. The result was rather like two animal stalls. Although both stalls had a front view, neither could see into the neighboring stall. In each stall I had put a chair, small table, ashtray, cigarettes, and a can of soda.

In the area in front of the stalls, I'd arranged four mattresses on the open floor and covered them with sheets. Off to one side was the building's tripod movie screen, which we kept for training, and on a small table stood a 16-millimeter projector set up with a very small roll of film. At this point, I had Paul sit in one of the stalls and put his blindfold in place. I tested it and then instructed him to sit there without a sound until I brought the other contestant in.

Placing my chair in front of the two stalls, I could now see both blindfolded victims, and neither of them could see the other. Both were now told to remove the eye masks.

The camp was closed, the property was chained, and the building was totally secured with a new inside sliding-bolt lock on the front door. The windows had been covered with thick pieces of cardboard held in place with tacks and duct tape. I was totally charged, and for a few seconds, I recall I felt I would be unable to speak. I took a swig of my own strong drink.

I began by saying that neither of them really knew if there was someone else on the other side of the tarp, and to prove that there was and that he was ready to play "Let's Make A Deal," each of them was to now strip to his undershorts, and toss all his clothing out onto the mattresses as proof of his being willing and ready. The boys quickly complied. Seeing them begin to enact what I had pictured in my mind for so many nights brought me to the point where my hands were actually shaking and my mouth was bone dry.

## TEST I

The first test was to get both to admit to all they had done. To accomplish this, I explained we would play a game of twenty questions. Each time that they answered a question, they would each receive one dollar. So, for twenty truthful answers, they would pick up twenty dollars spending money. I then had them put their blindfolds back on, and I led them to the mattresses. I told them that I would read out twenty questions regarding things that they may have done. After each question, each victim was to reach out and touch the other if he had done what had been asked. Seeing the two of them lying there next to each other blindfolded, precisely as I had envisioned it, was fascinating, and I then read the questions. In these, I ran the entire range from fondling to performing oral sex and included a question about being photographed. Both victims answered these correctly, truthfully, and both seemed surprised at how much the other had done.

## TEST II

After the initial test, I returned each boy to his separate stall. We had a smoke break with their blindfolds once again removed, and I handed each of them the cardboard sheet that showed the assortment of fishing tackle being offered as the next prize. This time they showed the other their willingness to continue the game by tossing their undershorts out onto the mattresses and save for the blindfolds, were now nude. After all the planning, manipulating, and fantasizing, I finally saw the two of them next to each other—naked and still not knowing who the other was.

I led them back to the mattresses, had them lie down, and explained that I would now give a series of instructions. If they both followed my directions quickly and with no difficulty, they would both vacation for two weeks and both get the extra fishing tackle.

I assigned them each a number, one and two, so that they could follow my exact instructions, and asked them to touch each other if they were ready to begin. When they did this, I then worked them through every sexual perversion that they had ever performed. It was at this point that my electric high exploded. I issued the first instruction and watched the two of them begin to perform, still not knowing the identity of their partner. This was a very long, slow process during which each of them was made to perform each act several times on the other. The conclusion of this session was having one boy perform oral sex on me, while the other used his hands to "see" what was happening and then having them change places. Now, each knew everything there was to know about the other, except who he was.

After returning to their individual stalls, and allowing

another brief smoke break, I informed them that there was yet another test and one that neither of them suspected. I carefully explained that they had both done great, and both had earned the two-week camping trip. I continued by saying that the final test was a special bonus, something I had figured out to reward them for having done so well up to this point.

The prizes for this test would be the biggest yet, but it was also going to be the most difficult for them. I made it clear that in order to win this test, both had to work together, each agreeing to do just a little bit more, not just for his own sake, but for the sake of the other guy. Then I explained the prizes and the final test.

## TEST III

The prizes for the third test were that each of them would receive the rod and reel set and an additional week of camping. But I made it clear that the third week of camping would only be awarded if both agreed. If one said yes, and the other said no, the cooperative one would receive the rod and reel, but neither would spend the third week in the mountains. To earn that, they had to work together.

I'd spent a tremendous amount of time trying to work out a speech that explained what I now demanded from them. But every time I worked on it, it was too long and too involved. I knew that I needed to deliver a shock and force a decision without allowing either of them too much time to think it through.

In one of my fantasy sessions, I envisioned a way that seemed to work. A picture, it seemed to me, was really going to be worth a thousand words. I placed the movie screen in a position where both victims could see it and said that I was about to show a quick movie in which they would see two boys about their own age and a third boy who was closer to seventeen or eighteen. I told them that they should think of these three actors as the three of us, and what the two younger boys were doing was exactly what each of them would agree to do in order to win the final prize. I added several lines about noticing how easily these two kids handled it all, and the fact that while the first time might seem strange, having your friend there and knowing that he was doing the same as you were, would make it all a lot easier for both of them.

When my sales pitch was finished, I said that when the film was done, each of them would get two minutes to decide, adding that knowing the two of them, it probably would take far less time to come to an answer. At the end of that two-minute period, I would shut off the light, making the room entirely black. When I did that, they were to do one of two things. If they agreed to do what they had seen, they would just walk out to the mattresses and stand there, without their blindfold or any clothing. If they chickened out, they would still walk out to the mattresses, but they would do so with their undershorts on. I then placed each of their undershorts inside their stalls, turned off the light, and ran the brief portion of film I had selected.

The film was one that I had purchased in the city, and it showed three boys sexually engaged with each other. In it, one victim was performing oral sex on one of the younger boys, while at the same time the older, teenage victim was anally sodomizing him. A minute or two later, the younger boys reversed places, so that both of them ended up being dually abused at the same time. In the closing shot, the youngest victim was shown letting the teenager ejaculate into his mouth.

When the three- or four-minute clip was done, I turned

on the lights and said that they now had two minutes to think it over. If either had the answer prior to that time, he was to raise his hand, and when both hands were raised, I would shut out the light. Then they would do as I had instructed: Give their answer and meet their mystery friend.

In a little more than a minute, both hands were raised. I told them I was going to kill the light, but I reminded them that what they decided right now not only affected themselves but also their friend. Then, with a very shaky hand, I switched off the light.

Every step of the entire ritual had been electrifying for me: watching both of my victims move through all that I had designed, exactly as I had pictured it. And from the moment they'd arrived, I had been totally caught up in what felt like the exercise of limitless power. I reminded myself that the first thing I wanted to see when light returned was not their shorts but the expression on their faces when they finally saw the other boy.

In the darkness, I heard them move forward. With a shaking hand, I threw the switch. Both boys were naked and both without their blindfolds. They seemed genuinely amazed at discovering whom the other was—relieved and happy with whom his mysterious partner turned out to be. I felt as if I totally owned both of them—their minds as well as their bodies. As I stood there watching these two naked children, I felt a level of control beyond anything I ever felt before.

I had not proven my power by raping them—something I would do the following night.

Yet even as I watched what I had spent so many hours fantasizing, another thought began running through my mind. For just a second, I pictured how totally exciting it would be to use both boys together with Paul's little brother. Even at the very instant an obsession was fulfilled, there was no end. For me, there would never be an end. At that precise moment, when I had everything, it still wasn't enough.

## Alan's Summary

It seems obvious to me that the degree to which each individual pedophile needs to validate his control in life plays a distinct part in the frequency and escalation of his acting out. As I believe this to be the case, I feel that the public's virtual preoccupation with the ultimate sexuality of the crime tends to prevent them from seeing, or addressing, the totality of the issue at hand. To defeat me, and others like myself, it is imperative for parents, educators, and other concerned individuals to broaden the scope of their understanding as to what forces motivate my actions and what techniques I employ in attempting to obtain my ends.

Unquestionably, control is not the only motivating force behind my acting out, but it is a powerful and extremely significant factor, one that I believe, for the most part, is missing in most people's understanding of pedophile's crimes. If I were driven by purely sexual motivation, it seems far more likely that I would have attempted to gratify my perverted obsession in a manner that would be much safer, such as using child prostitutes.

A mental state of victimization, a desperate compulsion to validate some form of personal control, an unquestionably perverted sexuality, the intentional distancing of ourselves from the real world, the progressive sexualization of our entire lives, and a sickening fascination with secrets, lies, and manipulations—all seem to be individual numbers in the combination. Numbers that, if used in the proper sequence, unlock the monster that we carry in our minds.

My acting out and my obsession were to continue for another twenty years. During that entire period, the frequency of my abusing and the extremes to which I went to carry out my abuses continually escalated.

I could quite easily write hundreds of pages on the growing array of sick, twisted abuses that occurred in the following years—instances where I forced friends to betray friends and brothers to betray brothers. Although the level of my abuse skyrocketed, the fundamental elements remained the same.

Pedophilia is no more an act of control than it is an act of sex or rage or any other single element. But I hope that from what I have written, you will see that the element of control is critical and is one that clearly needs to be understood if we are ever to deal effectively with pedophilia.

# CHAPTER TWENTY

*Amy:*

# Alan Gets Caught

Alan was eventually caught after a mother found a Polaroid of her son in a sexual position while she was cleaning his room. She contacted the police, Alan was apprehended, and charges were pressed. An investigation ensued, and many other victims came forward. Alan pleaded guilty on all charges. His charges numbered so high that he had the dubious distinction of being the largest-scale sexual offender in the area.

I attended his sentencing hearing. I remember the scene quite vividly. Alan, looking small and defeated, stood shackled before the judge in a courtroom that was shaped like an arena. The seating area formed a semicircle elevated above the trial proceedings. The layout of the room encouraged those in attendance to view themselves as an audience at a spectacle.

I was seated in the center, in the last row. To my far right were hordes of photographers and journalists talking excitedly. To my far left were dozens of victims and their families. Most of the victims were just reaching adolescence. Many were crying. Their fathers looked furious; their mothers seemed to be in shock. I was the only one sitting in the middle. No one else sat even near my section. I saw the media exchanging information and inquiries about my identity and purpose there.

When asked to speak, Alan uttered only a few quiet words of regret. I knew that he had originally planned to give a speech of remorse. I could only assume that he couldn't summon up the energy or the courage to read his lengthy script in its entirety. I felt a sense of defeat emanating from him. We both knew that he had several consecutive life sentences to face, with no option of parole.

The fact that he would die in prison was a given; how he would die we didn't know. Most likely, his death would be a violent one at the hands of fellow prisoners, as was often the case with sexual offenders. And because Alan was both middle aged and physically frail, this likelihood was even stronger. I also knew that his sentencing would mark the end of our sessions since he would be immediately moved to another facility. I felt a sense of loss, the closing of a chapter. I had a rented mailbox at the post office and had given the address to Alan, but I didn't know if or when he would write.

The hearing came to a close and Alan was given his sentence, five to six consecutive life sentences with no parole. He silently accepted, then shuffled out, still shackled, surrounded by guards. People on the victims' side of the courtroom began to hug each other, and tears of relief flowed freely down many parents' faces. Many of the boys now looked angry and threw punches in the air. The media began a feeding frenzy. Some of them rushed over to me. I quickly exited and walked numbly and silently to my car. It was easy to feel empathy for the victims of such terrible crimes, but this was the first time I felt my empathy open up to Alan, as well. I found myself reflecting on the isolation he must always feel.

Alan did, indeed, write me almost immediately after being transferred to the first of many long-term facilities. His letters varied enormously from dry, rather scholarly detached writings to emotionally-laden poems. Whatever the format, his letters offered me insights into the mind of a pedophile.

Alan had the unique experience of living with other incarcerated pedophiles for almost a decade while serving time on a sexual offenders unit. During this time, he spoke with them and recorded their conversations on paper. He analyzed their talks and their perceptions.

Alan has compared their experiences and invariably found similarity after similarity. His experiences, while frightening, are extremely relevant to an understanding of the enormity of the problem of pedophilia. His lengthy, detailed letters to me have chronicled the prison life of a pedophile. This correspondence includes testimony on the long-term effects of incarceration on pedophiles who are then released—information never before made public.

I have worked in prisons in several states during my career as a music therapist. Generally I have been on male maximum-security units, often limited to the criminally insane. Many elements are the same in all locations: the industrial gray floors and the metal furniture fastened to them seems to be made and shipped from one center in the country. All have a series of gates one must pass through to enter the unit, and rules and procedures accompany each one.

Even the feelings that I have on entering are consistent. While I am frisked and my instruments are searched, I feel impatient. When the gates clang loudly behind me, I feel a sense of claustrophobia. I am always relieved that I only choose to work at these types of facilities on a part-time basis and rarely enter more often than once a week. As I pass through halls of jeering men behind bars I feel ill at ease.

Once on the unit I am ultra-alert. I am often locked into a small day room with my patient or group of patients. Usually the guard is directly outside. I could have a guard with me, but it would compromise my work because it would virtually eliminate the chance that the men might open up about anything significant during the sessions.

I actually feel safer locked in this room than out in the area where explosions of violence are much more likely to occur. Perhaps it is because I am one of the few females on the unit and because I don't look like a typical corrections officer. The men seem to feel the need to maintain control over themselves to ensure my safety. Because the type of therapy I offer involves something pleasurable and important in their lives, I may also be part of a paired association of enjoyment. Prisoners often tell me that I am a reminder of their pasts, and for some of them, their futures. For whatever reasons, I have never been attacked.

I have witnessed some awful things in prisons, both between prisoners and between staff and prisoners. I remember walking into a unit once and knowing immediately from the silence that something was amiss. I opened the windowless door and looked around, simultaneously locking it behind me, as I had learned to do—sideways so that my back was never fully to the unit—and I realized that almost no one was in the common entry area. Only two men were near me, one heaped over on the floor and covered with blood, the other pacing in tight circles around him, holding something in his bloody hand. The staff was huddled behind the Plexiglas of an enclosed station a few steps to my right, watching me with mouths open. I decided to make a dash for that room rather than attempting to go back out the locked door, because I trusted my legs more than my hands. I also felt more secure knowing that if I raced for the station, I could watch the patient the entire time. Whereas if I went out the door, I would have to look at the lock before inserting my key. I made the dash and, fortunately, the inmate was too absorbed to look in my direction.

As soon as I made it into the station, the security force that had been called stormed into the common area dressed in riot gear. They quickly surrounded and shackled the patient. It turned out that he had attacked his victim with the razor blade that was still in his hand because he believed he heard voices telling him his fellow inmate was the devil. The victim survived.

As shocking as this was, it was less disturbing somehow than some other acts of violence I have witnessed. One of the saddest involved guards egging on a new sixteen-year-old inmate, telling him to walk up to another inmate (whom he actually liked) and punch him in the face. If he could break his nose with the punch, the new inmate would earn a pack of cigarettes. When I met him the next day, he was sitting, happily smoking. He felt no remorse, just wondered what else he could earn from the guards.

These acts of violence in prisons never triggered the nightmares I suffered when I witnessed violent acts on the outside, perhaps because I somehow felt less helpless in these situations. At least I could work with the instigators and victims—try to help them understand their actions and find other means of accomplishing what they needed to do emotionally. The music often afforded me an immediate way into their confidences.

I remember one particular patient who rarely spoke about anything other than his immediate surroundings, certainly never about his past. Instead, he was content to speak superficially about the meals or weather or television shows instead. He was blind in one eye, and the staff had never been told how he lost his eye. As we spoke about his favorite songs, he asked me to play the song, "Behind Blue Eyes," by the group entitled "The Who," on my guitar. After I sang the last stanza, he said to me that this song expressed exactly his situation. "No one knows what it's like behind my blue eye," he told me and then explained how he tore out his own eye after driving for days with the corpses of his wife and mother-in-law in his trunk. He had tied them both up, raped the mother-in-law in front of her daughter, then killed them both. He said that since he forced his wife to watch her own mother's torture and death, it was only fair for him to lose the ability to watch anything. "An eye for an eye," he told me. This song not only helped me and the rest of the staff to understand the severity of his condition, but it also launched his first honest talks about what else he had witnessed, done, and felt.

One of my patients, a teenage inmate serving a 20-year sentence, was an incredible musician. He wrote songs about his desire to molest young girls. Family members seldom visit forensic patients, but his mother came frequently. I met her during one of her visits and commented on his amazing musical talents. She broke down in sobs, explaining that no one had said anything "nice or even decent" about her son for the past ten years.

Many victims and much of the public feel that one's crimes define one's self. I honestly meant what I had said to the mother, since the music allowed me an additional view of her son. I was certainly concerned first and foremost with his crimes, but my additional musical connection to him afforded me a fuller view of him as a person.

In the excerpts from Alan's letters that follow, he struggles to maintain a connection with the other parts of himself, the ones outside of his pedophilia. Prison affords him (and others like him) time away from victims to consider these other parts of his humanity, but it can also erode them because of the cruelty of the prison surroundings.

Alan's letters cover a range of subjects, and I have presented many excerpts detailing his history as an abuser. Separated from all potential victims, he turned his natural capacity for analytical thinking away from devising manipulative plans to entrap victims and toward a fuller understanding of pedophilia. What follows reflects a genuine effort to find a healthy purpose in his life.

# CHAPTER TWENTY-ONE

## *Alan:*

# Life in Prison

*Two years after his arrest:*

I am writing this two years after my arrest. My room is about six feet wide and ten or twelve feet long. It has a window that overlooks one of the exercise yards. In the room, I have a small night table, a six-foot-high locker, a steel bed, no springs just a steel plate, and a small bookshelf over the bed. The room has been painted medium blue trimmed in black, but the paint has seen better days.

The floor is tiled, but again, the tile has reached the point where although you can keep it clean, keeping it shiny is impossible. For heat there are two pipes running through the room. One of them provides heat for roughly a ten-inch radius. During the winter, the window is covered with a plastic sheet held to the wall with masking tape. This helps but does not totally stop the winter wind from blowing in. Directly over my bed is a single sixty-watt light (no globe, just a light bulb), with a string leading down to the bed so that I can turn it off when I turn in. In short, this is not the most picturesque room that I have ever seen. It's rather dull, cold, and frequently windy, but I love it. It's private and in the middle of an ultra-institutional setting, *it's my space*! I guess you get the idea.

*Alan on his fellow inmates:*

I've concluded that you must begin to develop a "maximum" mentality if you are going to survive behind the wall. Respect is a primary factor in here. If someone thinks that you are not showing him respect, the result is, almost without exception, violence.

It's much like walking through a minefield. You learn to watch people and situations with extreme care and to listen to every word that is being spoken. To let down your guard is to expose yourself to real danger. You also find yourself thinking more in terms of defensive and offensive weapons. Everything that you see can be used to defend you, or if you are careless, used against you.

I am not becoming paranoid, just learning how to live in a very different environment. Others have to learn to adjust to going back on the outside, but I must learn the opposite. One of the things that I have going for me is the fact that I am a lifer. It is a predrawn conclusion that anybody who will be spending the rest of his life in prison will not hesitate to use a shank (knife) on you, if necessary, simply to eliminate you. And it's true. You think differently knowing that tomorrow is just going to be another day in prison. Again, not that you are looking for trouble, but you don't fear it. Win, lose, or draw, you will have to, and you will, defend yourself.

As far as my sexuality goes, I'm still gay. But I find not acting out my sexuality pretty easy in here. Mind you, the primary objects of my particular sexuality are not found in here, but even so, I don't feel overly attracted to any of the younger guys I encounter. Most of the time, I feel like a monk. It isn't that the possibility for acting out in here does not exist, for it does. Guys in here have few compunctions about having any variety of sex. And it isn't that the desire for physical contact doesn't still exist within me, for while I'm now fifty, I sure ain't dead. It's just that the insane compulsion and the exciting illegality of the game aren't there.

### Amy's Note:

After Alan was discovered, he fled to a unit at a hospital that specialized in treating pedophilia. There he was treated while awaiting his formal charges and incarceration.

### Alan four years after his arrest:

Looking back, I realize that it was not until I was put on Depo and later Lupron, (these are both drugs that inhibit or reduce the production of testosterone) that I had any feeling for what life could be without living under the constant pressure of sexual drives and desires. After two weeks on Lupron, my entire life truly changed. Ever since I was a preschool child, sex had been the predominant issue in my life. I cannot remember a period in my life when I was not acting out and spending endless hours lost in fantasy and plotting. Throughout the entire course of my life, nothing that I did proved sufficient to break this destructive obsession until I was put on Lupron.

Obviously, Lupron, or any other form of chemical castration, does not alter the mind's ability to conjure up deviant thoughts. But at least in my personal experience, the thoughts, without the ability to achieve gratification, are short lived and reach a point of virtually ceasing to exist. The most stimulating and erotic of ideas has little appeal when the body refuses to respond. For the first time, I could go to sleep at night without fantasizing and masturbating, and I could watch television without being turned on by every young boy I caught sight of.

As strange as it sounds, I could actually see the world

around me and feel like I'm a legitimate part. I can't tell you how many times I lay in bed at night asking myself what life could have been like if I had been given this drug twenty or thirty years earlier.

There is absolutely no question in my mind that for people who know that they need this medication, it should be both allowed and encouraged. But the Lupron is only effective if you continue to administer it. If, at any given time, you decided, for any given reason, to discontinue the medication, you would find yourself right back where you were. I knew that I would have to spend the rest of my life on medication—particularly if I was not indicted and imprisoned. I also knew that there was always the possibility that somewhere down the line I just might be tempted to change my mind and experience what life would be like without the drug. After a long and almost sleepless night, I agreed to physical castration and signed the necessary forms.

Unfortunately, prior to the operation, my indictment came down, and I was returned, intact, to the state. For the entire period that I was in a county jail, I was allowed to take Lupron, but when I was remanded into state custody the medication was stopped. When this happened, I returned to my previous state and for the past four years, have had to fight a constant war against fantasy and masturbation. I don't think that a day passes without wishing that my arrest had not taken place before the operation was performed. Had such been the case, that is, had I had the procedure, my life, even here in prison, would be immeasurably easier and far more worthwhile.

Castration is the loss of your sexual being, but at least for people like me, it is the only sane choice for living. In extreme cases like mine, I don't think there is any question regarding the morality or the legality of having this procedure performed.

Who in their right mind would not be willing to surrender one aspect of their being to save their life? A person with cancer will readily submit to the amputation of a limb in order to survive.

The difficulty with this issue comes with regard to the state's right to mandate castration. The issues relative to legislated castration are complex. I am for voluntary castration as a means of allowing life for extreme cases, but I have many reservations regarding the use of mandated procedures. The procedure, on one hand, can be an enlightened and effective tool for saving the life of a dangerous offender and the lives of his victims, but it can also be used legally as a means of revenge, punishment, and anger venting.

### *Alan five years after his arrest:*

The prison physician determined that I needed to undergo some complicated medical testing, so I was escorted (shackled, of course) to a nearby community hospital. Most of the guys in here enjoy nothing more than having the opportunity to get back out into the world, if even briefly. I don't! It remains for me a world that I simply can't handle. A world of conflicting emotions, and above all, a world populated with kids. As they were taking me from the transport van into the hospital I had to walk directly past a very attractive, blond-haired, eleven- or twelve-year-old boy. That was all I needed. All of the old feelings came crashing down. I felt as if this kid was a magnet pulling me mentally toward him. I knew that I couldn't stare at him, particularly with the guards present (they know what I'm in for, don't like it, and it wouldn't take too much to give them an excuse to act out on their own).

The entire incident could not have taken more then a minute. But in those sixty seconds, I saw again what I really am. I felt those same sickening feelings and went immediately into a deep, twisted, violent fantasy. I hate this, but it is me, or such a major part of me that it feels as if it were all of me. Perhaps the best result of all this is that at least I recognize that I am still a very sick, twisted, and dangerous individual. I am not so foolish as to believe that I had somehow become cured. I had no delusion about being free of pedophilia, but I had not come in contact with anything in the last couple of years that caused me to react in the old manner. I didn't even slow down. I saw, I wanted, and if I were free, I would most likely have sought a manner of acting out. It really threw me, and I am far from being over it now.

Even as this brief incident was taking place, I could not help but be taken aback by the situation. Here I was in leg irons, in handcuffs, with my cuffs chained to my waist, confronting exactly the type of child who got me here in the first place. Now, even under these hideous circumstances, I wanted that kid.

In spite of all that has taken place, and knowing more about myself and my illness than I have ever known before, in spite of knowing that I will spend the rest of my life behind four-foot-thick granite walls, all I could think of was that I wanted that boy.

Nothing has changed. The intensity of the urge, the overwhelming mental leap into fantasy, and the physical response of the body were, as they have always been, overactive. No, I did not expect that I had become a new man or that my pedophilia had gone away, but I did anticipate that there would be some difference in the way I saw things. None! All of my attack systems were immediately operative, fully ready to do what I have always done.

I saw this kid five days ago, and I am still very much fighting fantasy. He has become part of my dreams. I sexually and physically abuse this unknown boy to the ultimate degree possible. In this dream, I sense no guilt, no conflict, or remorse, just pure acting out in every sense of the word. I know full well that dreams can't hurt other people, but they do cause the dreamer a great deal of pain.

If nothing else, I am now more glad than ever that I am tightly confined behind large walls and iron bars. I look out at the endless rows of barbed ribbon wire fences and am honestly glad that they are there. Although there is a tiny part of me that wants freedom, I am comforted by the knowledge that it can't and will never be a part of my future. Unfortunately, I am one of those individuals who can only really exist in total confinement. I don't argue with this. And I have no desire to face temptation again. Oh yes, I hate prison, and I know full well that the worst is yet to come,when I will be placed back in with the mainstream of prisoners, but it's a whole lot better than what would happen were I back on the streets again.

### Alan six years after his arrest:

The present, for me, is a state of attempting to find ways in which I feel some purpose is still possible for me. Prison is a void, a dehumanizing process in which individuals are warehoused until some given point in time and then returned to society. Rehabilitation is, to a very large degree, a joke that is perpetuated to placate the public.

Like a survivor, the offender's struggle is continual and tough. And while I don't mean to make a comparison between the suffering of the innocent survivors and the hardships of the offenders, I do want to let you know that when we decide to fight the monsters in our mental closet, it's one hell of a fight.

So much of our identity rests in our acceptance of ourselves as being perverts. The ultimate justification for always giving in to our desires is the old, "Why not? That's all you really are." At such a young age, the offender, at least this offender and a lot of others whom I have encountered, cease to see ourselves as anything but perverts. In part this is because we feel no orientation with the rest of the world. This provides us with an all-purpose justification for doing anything we want.

At least now I have gained enough insight to see that there is more to me than just the monster my perverted sexuality leads me to be. And, strangely, knowing and really believing that there is more to me than my depraved sexuality helps to provide me with both incentive and strength to keep myself under control. I could only begin to grow when I really believed that there was any part of me capable of growing, capable of saving, and capable of engendering within me a desire to grow.

How do I feel right now? Well, I have pedophilia, but I won't continue to let it have me, not all of me, and not at anyone else's expense. I also know that despite my emotional sickness, there is good in me and the ability to take control of things that I never dreamt were controllable. I don't feel whole, but I don't feel like the totally broken, dirty, and worthless thing I always saw myself as ...

I'm still spending a lot of time talking to other offenders and a *lot* of time writing. I really believe that a part of the "paying back" that I need to do is tied in with my attempting to work with other offenders while I have the chance and to write as much about this issue from the offender's point of view as I can. If I can say something to another offender, or write something that means anything to them, to prevent their ending up as I have, then I do serve a purpose.

No, I won't be back out there, and I won't do a lot of the things that I have done in the past. After all, most of what I've done has been pretty screwed up and extremely destructive. I really don't mind the fact that my physical freedom is gone, but I absolutely must maintain some meaningful sense of purpose. On a scale of zero to 100, I think that I'm holding a pretty good fifty to sixty as far as my emotional balance goes, and given my circumstances, that "ain't bad at all."

### *Alan seven years after his arrest:*
This will be my seventh Christmas incarcerated, and as the months and years roll past, it does have an effect on you. When I sit down to write to someone on the outside, I find that most of the things that transpire behind these walls simply don't lend themselves to civil correspondence, not even to someone whom I trust as much as I do you. In addition to this, the few things which do seem appropriate for inclusion in a letter are totally boring, overtly mundane, and after several years of letter writing, unquestionably repetitious.

When I write to you, I attempt to keep the letters from being just frustration vents. I don't want to do what I see so many inmates doing: to send out envelopes filled with self-pity, frustration, and jailhouse horror stories. In my efforts to "sanitize" my correspondence, however, I often find myself faced with the task of writing about nothing. What I have discovered lately is that writing this type of controlled correspondence heightens my frustration with my current circumstances. I sit here trying to find civil topics of conversation, and that exercise focuses me more intensely on the emptiness of this environment.

Well, I would be less then honest if I didn't say that I have my definite ups and downs, not critical lows, mind you, but some periods where all of the futility of incarceration really gnaws away at me.

Let me attempt to describe for you the mental battle that plays a major portion in my current role. When a person is sent to prison and accepts the reality that he is not going to be getting out again, he loses one of the major elements of life: time. It is the elastic band that links our past to our present and measures our progress toward some distant point, event, goal, etc. When there is no longer something concrete to be measuring toward, your entire concept of time is suddenly shattered. It is as if this device is now only useful for determining the distance from something, not to it.

My daily battle is not with the administration or with the rules and regulations, nor do I sit and waste time feeling that society has done me any form of injustice (i.e., a much longer sentence than most of the men in here for abuse offenses). My battle lies in that subtle area called personal motivation, the ability to find and maintain a sense of purpose that allows you to continue seeing yourself as a whole being.

I guess what I'm trying to say is that when you know that you're not going anywhere, your daily battle is to make where you are mean something. I read endlessly, write (particularly about addiction, pedophilia, and the commonality that I see in the lives of those who have ended up here), type endless letters for guys who need a hand in putting their ideas down on paper, teach in our school (where, I might add, my two students are doing very well), tutor at night, paint, draw, talk to anyone who is interested in working on creating change in their lives, and, I'm even slowly learning to be a reasonably good listener with an open mind, never one of my strong points. In addition to that, I do some writing for the chaplain, i.e., writing his annual appeal letter and a follow-up thank-you letter. I do a great deal of inventory work in the building, polish the brass doorknobs, wash tables, and do just about anything else that provides me with some sense of self-worth.

The problem arises when I hit those periods when all of this seems like just so much fluff and no substance. When you shut the light off at night and take a mental inventory of the day, you then realize that this is, in a very real way, the totality of your present and future existence. Here the old concept of time rears its ugly head, and you have a sweeping, sickening feeling of perpetual nothingness. And when that mood arises, it really takes every bit of my mental and physical energies to fight it. *But* I do.

One of the strongest weapons I have found in this battle is the realization that I live in a world where I must create meaning and purpose, and then stop and make myself appreciate the fact that everybody does, regardless of where they are or what they are doing. I have to constantly remind myself that when I was on the outside I was totally free but equally meaningless. Normally, by putting things back into some type of perspective, i.e. looking at what I accomplished on the streets, I am able to see that all of life is going to be whatever I choose to make of it. And when I reset the mind, clear out the self-pity, frustration, and depression, I am once again ready to find satisfaction in such things as writing a new poem, talking to a young offender, or, yes, even polishing an old doorknob.

### Alan on rehabilitation:

In your moving letter, you stressed the importance of both therapy and support groups, and in this regard, I could not agree with you more. When I was in the hospital, on the special perpetrator unit, my doctor took me, on two occasions, to sit in on one of his outpatient support groups for sex offenders. At these meetings, he constantly stressed the belief that it was the group and not just his professional presence that brought forth the real promise of help. He took great pains to reinforce his belief that his role was that of technical advisor, but the bulk of the benefit to be derived from group participation lay in the sharing of common feelings, experiences, and addictions.

Each of us, the victims and the offenders, lives in our own world of personal isolation. How frequently it appears that this sense of isolation is one of the motivators in an offender's acting out, and how frequently the result of his abuse is a victim being traumatized into his or her own world of guilt-ridden and dirty-feeling isolation. I have seen more genuine progress made with the offenders whom I have come into contact with simply through the process of being surrounded by peers and therefore having to face the reality that they are neither alone nor different from other offenders.

Until I actually came into contact with other pedophiles and began to feel a sense of commonality and yes, even acceptance, I could read and listen to the news stories about molestation and mentally distance myself from them. In fact, although I am not proud to admit it, I frequently used that type of news item as a means for feeding my own sexual desires and fantasies. But it's different when you are actually face to face with another offender. To illustrate what I am speaking of, let me share with you a very typical example of what goes on in some programs for sexual offenders.

Ted (not his actual name) is a guy about thirty-two years old. He is here serving time for sexually abusing both his stepsons. The abuse consisted of forcing the boys to perform oral sex and, finally, forcing the older child (then age twelve) to submit to anal abuse. Not a pretty story but not uncommon in here.

When I first sat down with Ted, he flatly refused to see, or even examine, the fact that he was sexually attracted to his stepsons. In his mind, what he had done was a form of discipline arising from his anger with the children for their behavior. He clung desperately to the view that this was "just another form of discipline," and while he would concede that it was an "unusual" and "perhaps extreme" measure, he would in no way see it as having any sexual component.

I let him know my views relative to his behavior, that he was a pedophile and that his actions demonstrated not only a perverse sexual attraction but also a very sadistic streak. I told him that he should consider himself lucky for having been caught before be accidentally killed one or both of those boys.

Ted and I didn't have another in-depth conversation for six months. During the time, I was a member of both his large and small therapy groups, and we frequently did battle on these issues in those forums. Fortunately for Ted, not only was he involved in ongoing group therapy sessions, but he was surrounded by perverts. Everywhere he turned, he was forced in one way or another to see himself. How did he reach the point of finally beginning to see his own actions in the light of reality? Well, he could easily ignore the therapists, but what he couldn't ultimately ignore was seeing himself and hearing his words in those around him.

It's pretty hard to pretend that you're different from other offenders when you sit and listen to them use the same words, lines, logic, and lies that you have used with your victims for so many years. I can tell you from personal experience that one of the biggest shocks I have received was the first time that I heard another pedophile repeat, almost verbatim, the words that I so often used in my seduction process, only it was his process! The impact of that experience is mind boggling simply because you realize that if the words and the logic are the same, then so is the illness, the criminality, and the ultimate damage to the victim(s).

When Ted began to see and accept the fact that he was not different from us but rather very much one of us, his world began to change. I think that the therapists and doctors could have talked to him forever and not broken through the ancient defensive wall of "being different." They couldn't break through it because they couldn't share with him the unique language and feelings of an abuser. Ted came literally very, very close to killing the oldest boy, and yet he refused to see that his sexual, sadistic behavior was escalating. Now things that he did not want to look at or remember, such as the incidental use of a belt and his fists and the gradual increasing infliction of real physical pain against the boys, are becoming clear to him. He is beginning to really see that he was attacking them in every conceivable way, sexually, physically, mentally, and emotionally, and his frustration, perversion, and anger were steadily pushing him to greater depths.

Ted is a sick man, and far from being cured (if such a state were ever obtainable), but at least now, he is more in touch with the reality of his sickness and more willing to face it head on. I attribute a tremendous amount of his progress to the fact that he has been surrounded by "peers," combined with professional guidance. So, I, too, firmly believe that peer groups for both survivors and offenders are a critical part of the overall recovery process.

# CHAPTER TWENTY-TWO

## *Alan:*
# Pedophilia After Incarceration

I am constantly amazed at just how quickly the time passes in here. I have been in this sexual offenders program for four years, and yet it really seems as if I arrived only weeks ago. One of the disheartening aspects of being here for so long is watching so many of the guys get released, only to learn a short time later that they are once again back in custody.

As this program deals primarily with alcoholics, drug addicts, and sex offenders, and as the people in this program have already demonstrated that they have no rigid personal boundaries in life, I suppose that this high level of reoffenders should not strike me as all that unusual. Still, it is a sad thing to watch. I guess in a way I am amazed that when a person is given another chance, an opportunity to live beyond the dehumanizing, brutal, and depressing confines of the walls that surround us, he still can't find it in himself to control his behavior.

I have been reflecting on the various individuals who I have known here, those who have been released and very quickly found their way back, and I have come up with the following observations concerning their behaviors. I think that I would break the reoffending ex-cons into three major classifications: those who just really didn't care about their lives and used their time in this program as nothing more than a means of providing themselves with a comfortable place to do time; those who were genuinely concerned about reoffending, but because they were tightly confined and thereby deprived of their drug of choice (either alcohol, drugs, or sexual objects), began to think of themselves as "cured," and didn't feel that it was necessary to put the needed work into preparing themselves for reentry into a world filled with temptations; and those who never actually came to realize that they had a problem.

I would divide this final group into two subgroups: those who simply refused to accept any real responsibility for their previous behavior and preferred to "justify" their distorted thinking and actions by blaming circumstances, other people, fate, etc.; and those who learned to master the therapy game.

These offenders are the ones who learned all of the correct theories, phrases, words, and attitudes of the recovery program but failed to internalize any of their knowledge. They viewed the entire process as a sort of survival game, and in their distorted view of life, in order for them to survive in a confrontational program such as this one, they learned, all too quickly, what to say. Unfortunately, they saw all of this as only a game, and, while they learned to play this twisted little game extremely well, they failed to develop any real insights or controls that they needed for returning to society.

The second type of reoffending ex-cons are those who have recognized that they have a sickness but have been lured into a false sense of security by being confined in an environment that is devoid of temptation. Here again, I see a failure to totally accept the permanent nature of their sickness as the major cause of their ultimate reoffending. During the course of their incarceration, many in this group of offenders have learned a great deal about pedophilia, but they have failed to understand that learning about the illness is not a substitute for working daily to keep it under control.

As a result of having spent a significant amount of time locked away from children, they felt that their pedophilia is a thing of the past. Given the lack of available stimuli, they find the compulsiveness of their sickness greatly reduced. They may have even developed enough self-discipline to avoid watching TV programs and movies that would trigger them.

To varying degrees, some may have also brought their fantasies and masturbation under control (which some find significantly easier to do when there is an absence of children). In this unreal environment, they begin to believe what they so desperately want to believe: that they have finally brought their sickness to an end, that they are cured.

In essence, what this group of offenders is doing is finding another means of justifying their not having to do what others are forced to do. Again, they are seeing themselves as being different and therefore freed from the need to continue working on their recovery. A high percentage of these offenders have real difficulty in dealing effectively with their peers, a major factor in their being attracted to children, and yet they don't see any real connection between this inability on their part and the commission of their crimes.

They have now a new, acceptable justification for not having to force themselves to interact with those around them (at least some of them have); they can retreat to the isolation of their rooms and bury themselves in books that deal with theories on pedophilia or religious philosophy. Their defense of their actions now takes on almost moral proportions. After all, "how can you possibly fault me when I am devoting hours to studying my problem or pursuing my religious beliefs?"

To my mind, this form of escapism is absolutely deadly. Their adamantly clinging to written theories and religious offerings amounts to little more than a sophisticated continuation of their denial that a problem exists. Most of these men willingly admit that they are guilty of having offended but are very quick to point out that all of that was before they had either understood the sickness or found God, and of course, both groups will absolutely assure you that it could never happen again. Unfortunately, statistics prove they are wrong.

The good part of all of these thoughts that I have looked at, is the realization that I can see myself in each category. In all of the various defenses and distortions that I have talked about, I see my own behavior. I say that this is good because it helps me to see my own commonality, and it also lets me know that I am not treating all of this as some sort of academic exercise but rather a very personal quest.

# CHAPTER TWENTY-THREE

# The Public and Pedophilia

*Amy:*

What follows is an unprecedented discussion of the ramifications of proposed legislation calling for the death penalty for pedophiles. Soon-to-be-released pedophiles have been speaking in no uncertain terms with Alan about what they will now begin to do to protect their secrets, the lengths to which they will now go in order to silence their victims. And not only are those victims at risk, but inadvertent witnesses are also at risk, as is anyone with suspicions about the pedophile's crimes. It is crucial that we pay attention to the implications of pedophilia legislation for it affects us all.

Megan's Law has tremendous impact on both the public and the pedophile. There is frequent news coverage of the reactions of communities to the disclosure of the proximity of released convicts. Public outrage is wide and can be inflammatory. I find this legislation troubling and complex. Its position implies that pedophiles do not reenter society rehabilitated and that the prison experience does little to deter the offender from offending again.

In a sense it amounts to an extension of a prison sentence that the criminal pedophile has already served since listed sex offenders are ostracized from their communities. A fresh start is certainly out of the question for a former offender listed according to the requirements of Megan's Law. Yet what are we to do? Pedophiles are not being cured in prison, and out of prison our children are at risk.

Every time a child is molested, ripples of consequences touch many lives. You may not be aware that you know victims, but in all likelihood you do. He may disrupt your class. She may steal from your store. He may vandalize your car. She may molest your own child while baby-sitting. And of course, the consequences become dire once the victim grows to adulthood. These former victims become even more of a danger to themselves and others. One of Alan's victims grew to desire boys so strongly that he married a woman he didn't love in order to have access to her son.

Alan's letters to me contained many serious discussions about the way in which public perception played into his own gradual isolation. He makes a convincing plea for recognizing pedophilia as a disease first and foremost even before it is considered a crime.

The state in which Alan is incarcerated has an inmate population in excess of sixty thousand, approximately ten percent is estimated to include sexual offenders. He was fortunate enough to spend much of his sentence thus far in a special sexual offenders unit, which protects inmates from the ostracization and abuse they would receive in a regular unit.

This special unit has a maximum capacity of only 150 participants. Alan describes the horrendous experience that young prisoners had before coming to the unit and often reminded me in his letters of how many other kids (under the age of twenty) there were like them, many of whom would remain among the 5,850 who never get a place on the special unit.

## *Alan on his fellow inmates:*

The young men (virtually kids) who arrive here on the sexual offenders unit share one thing in common: They have young bodies and old, defeated eyes. Their eyes reflect the unspeakable experiences of their previous incarceration and the total hopelessness of their current state. A young man who has been gang raped and then handed from "owner" to "owner," who has been forced to perform any service or act just to stay alive, is not a candidate for reentering society as a productive citizen. What he has been forced to endure will ultimately result in his retaliatory abuse of innocent children.

It seems as if we live in a circle of pain. The public and the courts refuse to see pedophilia as a real emotional illness. A first-time teenage pedophile is often treated as if he were a casehardened and lifelong criminal. Members of the public call for the stiffest possible sentence, never realizing that by doing so, they are enlarging the overall problem. They delude themselves into thinking that imprisonment will teach the pedophile a lesson, and once he has had to sit in a cell for a few years, he will see the error of his ways. They expect the experience of incarceration will scare him to the degree that he will come out a cured and productive member of society. *Wrong!*

Imprisonment is not and can never be a substitute for therapy. On top of this, imprisonment in a system that turns a blind eye to the repeated brutal treatment of young pedophiles does nothing but instill within them a sense of rage. A person who is beaten, raped, and abused while incarcerated from the age of sixteen to nineteen or twenty reenters society a walking time bomb. He is still very much a pedophile, only now he is a pedophile seeking revenge against what he sees as a sadistic and unjust world.

I have heard of two different cases, both of which were young pedophiles subjected to abusive behavior during the period of their imprisonments. Both of these guys were released from prison. Shortly after their releases, both of them acted out sexually against young boys. In both cases, the victims of their second, postrelease crimes ended up being murdered. In these two cases alone, two deaths could possibly have been prevented, and the futures of two men altered, if only society had sought prevention instead of punishment.

More and more I am convinced that the only way that we will ever begin to deal effectively with the issue of child abuse is through public reeducation. The issue of pedophilia, which has too often been swept under the rug, must be brought to light and addressed in a realistic, concerned manner if we are ever to make any headway in preventing the abuse of our children.

### *Alan on the budding pedophile:*

The public is horrified by what we pedophiles do, and rightly so. People are concerned about the safety of their children, but in their anger, they act out in a manner that neither satisfies their taste for revenge nor ensures their children's safety. Stone walls and iron bars do not help sick people to gain control of themselves. The public attitude concerning pedophiles offers the potential offender no hope for help. How can a kid who knows that he has what seems like an uncontrollable attraction for sexual involvement with younger children, but lives in a society that only seeks to imprison and destroy people with those feelings, ever be encouraged to seek help before he begins to act out?

When I was fourteen or so, and knew that I had a major problem, I also knew that there was no place to turn. My one parent who was aware of the problem simply did not know how to handle it and ended up refusing to admit that the problem existed. Had I admitted to other adults that I had fantasies and thoughts of unnatural sexual activities with little children, I would have been marked for life as some sort of freak and virtually cast out of society. For a teenage or younger pedophile today, nothing has changed.

If a kid admits to having a problem with drugs or alcohol, the public is willing to see the addiction as a sickness and offer help. But for a kid to admit that he is a pedophile puts him in a position where even his own family will see him as a defective human.

In time you come to feel so alone, so angry at being nothing more than a broken piece of humanity, and so totally hopeless, that you attempt to relieve the pain and isolation by involving yourself with the only people who you don't see as a threat, children. Even if this involvement is, at first, of a nonsexual nature, you ultimately end up choosing to cross all the boundaries and act out. You hear your peers and adults making jokes or demanding the imprisonment or worse for child molesters, so you do everything within your power to hide the fact that they are talking about you. By fifteen years of age or so, all you know is that something is radically wrong with you and that it is so bad that you can't ever bring it to anyone's attention.

Sooner or later that isolated and confused teenager acts out, gets caught, and if unlucky, ends up being remanded to the custody of the state department of corrections.

Admittedly, sometimes a court does not incarcerate a very young offender but instead mandates therapy and releases him into the custody of his family. Unfortunately, the administrative load on the probation department and the courts is so heavy that following up on something minor like sex therapy for a young kid is not a priority.

Frequently, the offender is returned to a family situation where there is little if any support and a greater desire to hush the whole thing up than there is to support the boy through the process of therapy. Many parents simply can't face the reality that their child is sick, particularly that he is sick in such a dirty and unacceptable way. In a lot of these cases, some of which I have encountered in prison, therapy is never obtained for the young offender, and as a result, a year or so later at, let's say the age of sixteen, he offends again and finds himself back in court.

At this point, the court is through being "nice" to this kid. It is reasoned that the last time when he was given "every opportunity" to straighten himself out, he did nothing. So, the sixteen-year-old is finally made a part of the state prison system.

If he is lucky, and no one discovers the nature of his crime, he will only be subjected to the normal level of brutality that thrives in the prison environment. However, should someone recognize him or should one of the corrections officers read his file and out of a sense of disgust inform the other inmates about the nature of his crime(s) ... welcome to hell.

Because of his age, the court has most likely given him a relatively short sentence, but because of his crime, that moderate period of time will almost certainly be one continuous nightmare. As a young and usually withdrawn kid, he is a target to begin with. Once who he is becomes known, he will almost certainly be forced to live in a world of twisted, painful sex, violence, and constant terror, all of which just further distort his already confused view of life. Suicide is a constant preoccupation until he either attempts it or accepts the fact that he can't do it and submits to the brutality of the system.

Sooner or later this young man gets released. He is back in a world that he doesn't understand, driven by obsessions that he can't control, and feeling very alone. His family may be supportive, but by this stage of his life, he no longer trusts anyone.

His own pain, anger, and bitterness are explosive. All of his insecurities and all of the pressures that heightened his pedophilia to begin with are still there and now a thousand times stronger. His fear and distrust of the adult world are still there and now are supported by the reality of his own experience with the courts and prisons. With all of these factors stored up in him, he is released and told to stay out of trouble. He is only sure of one thing in life: He never wants to have to go back to jail, under any circumstances. At this point, with no help and no hope in sight, this kid's illness is at its most dangerous level.

# CHAPTER TWENTY-FOUR

## *Alan:*

# Punishment for Pedophiles

I believe that the proposed sentencing of all pedophiles to life imprisonment would escalate the panic-driven reactions that they have following the commission of a crime. I think that in an understandable attempt to protect its children, the public may well be blindly placing many, many innocent young lives at a significantly increased risk.

If I was willing to go to these extremes to avoid detection for a crime that carried a relatively small penalty, you can imagine the panic, fear, and the lengths to which I could be driven to avoid detection if the penalty on conviction was life. When I was in my distorted world of fantasy and escalation, knowing that the penalty had been increased would not have stopped me at all. At that stage, all I wanted was the object of my obsession, and the penalty had no place in my compulsive thought pattern.

If the penalty for molesting is life in prison and the penalty for murder is the same, then the panic-stricken mind of an already unstable man is likely to see he has nothing to lose by murdering the only witness to his crime. Because the vast majority of pedophiles would not [ordinarily] consider taking a victim's life, is it truly in the best interest of society to create a situation wherein that thought might be generated by fear of this enhanced punishment?

Another proposal would mandate a life sentence without parole for three-time violent offenders. Some of the public would assume that knowing such a sentence is hanging over your head would automatically keep you from ever even considering offending again. But that's just not a realistic expectation. I do feel for the victims of our crimes, and I really do believe that pedophiles must be stopped, but in a lot of cases, the third-time offender is going to be some nineteen- or twenty-year-old screwed-up kid who, despite the nature of his previous convictions, has never been offered any real help.

One of the younger prisoners here is a nineteen-year-old. He is a pedophile who has two felony convictions for sexual offenses. This kid's family, following his first felony conviction at sixteen didn't even bother to participate in any level of therapy with him, nor did they even see to it that he had transportation to and from therapy or the means to pay for it. They just didn't care enough. Therapy was a condition of probation, but the state didn't bother to follow up and take action when he stopped attending.

The obvious result was that in a couple of months, he was offending again, arrested again, and this time the court decided, "They had given him enough breaks." So this time he was sent to adult prison (at seventeen). I don't have to provide all of the details of what happened. A seventeen-year-old, small, blond, blue-eyed kid arrives in a state prison and either submits or dies. He didn't die. If the system had put this young man into decent therapy the first time he offended, and even

tried with him again on the second offense, then I could readily see his long-term incarceration as necessary. But is it fair to
put an emotionally disturbed teen in prison for life, without
the possibility of parole, without really attempting to provide
him with a means of first turning his life around?

The typical pedophile is not a sadist. Although he com-
mits hideous acts upon innocent children, the overwhelming
majority of child molesters do not "physically" abuse their
victims (in the conventional sense) nor do they even consider
the possibility of murdering them. What concerns me regarding the current proposed changes in the law is that even the
mildest of individuals, when suddenly faced with the fear and
panic of having offended, is likely to snap. The public likes to
believe that lengthening the time of incarceration will serve
as a deterrent to our acting out. I have little faith in that being
the case.

Once a person is wrapped up in the throes of his acts,
once the drives have reached the point where he is bordering
on being out of control, there is no thought given to possible
consequences. If the person involved were capable of sitting
rationally and weighing the pros and cons of the issue at
hand, there would most likely not be a need for offending. For
the act is not carried out in an environment of calm logic but
rather in a driven state of justifications, minimizations, delu-
sions, and denials. In such a state, it is not logical that an
obsessed individual is going to be moved by possible consequences.

I feel that this proposed law that is supposed to protect
children is far more likely to place many of them at significantly greater risk. I believe that the answer, if there really is
such a thing, lies in helping the offender deal with and control
his sickness and spending a much greater amount of time

working to educate children as a means of providing them with the type of self-confidence, knowledge, and skills needed to avoid being entrapped by someone like me.

I realize that my presentation here is an oversimplification of the issue. There are many factors to be taken into consideration at the time of sentencing, and some crimes must be dealt with in a harsh and protective fashion. Nor do I mean to imply that lifelong, repeat offenders should be treated with understanding and consideration. But in this cycle that presently exists, everybody ends up getting hurt. There must be a better way.

# CHAPTER TWENTY-FIVE

## *Amy:*
# Handling Sex Offenders

What is the best way to handle sexual offenders? I don't have the answer. I only know, both professionally and personally, what doesn't work. In prisons, I see only more street-savvy molesters being released. I believe that stringent therapy, combined with custody of child molesters, is the best shot we have at protecting our children and addressing the epidemic of sexual abuse that continues to afflict our society.

I know that we still have a lot of work to do in terms of detecting abuse and identifying sexual offenders, and that if we continue to be limited in our beliefs about the characteristics of potential suspects, we will continue to live in denial, and our children will continue to be at risk. I also know that unless we can entice molesters to seek help, we will never stop sexual abuse.

Alan once sought help for his pedophilia. Coincidentally, it was at a psychiatric hospital where I worked, but his hospitalization was long before I began to work there. Once he had checked himself onto the unit, he was interviewed. He was asked many questions but none regarding his sexuality. Had there been any such questions, perhaps he could have spoken up about what kind of help he desperately needed. Instead, he pleaded depression and was soon released without ever speaking about his problem. Unless an individual is directly asked and given permission to discuss his sexuality, it is extraordinarily unlikely for that person to reveal himself.

He felt that he was too much of a monster to receive any help. After this experience, he felt he was beyond help. He resorted to resigning himself to his fate and went on to abuse many more children over many years.

My doctoral dissertation focused on adults who had psychiatric illnesses as well as histories of sexual abuse. Finding volunteers to participate in my research was quite simple: A huge majority of those with mental problems have also been abused. All I needed to do was to ask the right questions. However, staff at most psychiatric hospitals don't ask about sexual abuse. They ask about drug or alcohol use, hearing voices, thoughts of killing oneself or others. I'm not suggesting that having been abused leads one directly into a mental hospital but rather that it is essential to inquire about what may be hidden, like sexual abuse. Few are likely to volunteer their personal involvement or experiences.

I certainly felt reluctant to speak up for many years. My worst fear was that people would assume that since I had been sexually abused, I would, in turn, molest my own children. I could have also feared that since my father and his family were alcoholics, people would assume that I, too, would become an alcoholic. But negative role models and experiences can be positive teachers. Knowing the dangers of alcohol made me decide to never use alcohol as a coping device.

The same consciousness exists in my relationship with my

children. Because of my experience of being victimized, I am the type of mother who is concerned with protecting my children, helping them become empowered to own their bodies actively, and respecting their boundaries and privacy. But my ability to speak up about my sexual abuse took much time, therapy, education, and support.

I was lucky to have had the chance to heal.

I know how my professional colleagues feel about my work with sexual offenders. The primary feelings they express about this population are distaste, disgust, and disdain. I believe that an underlying fear causes these feelings to surface. We fear what we don't know; we can't fix what we don't understand.

These peers who express this shock and repulsion ostensibly work with other populations, but for all they know, they too are working with molesters. The subject not discussed. When I speak about my other patients—victims of sexual abuse, children with brain tumors, adolescents with eating disorders, adults injured in accidents—many people with whom I have come in contact from the general, nonprofessional public praise my work and express empathy for my patients. But I don't hear expressions of public gratitude for my work with sex offenders. The most common reaction is silence.

I too, of course, am a member of the public. I grew up in American society. And I too have personal feelings regarding pedophilia. Strong feelings, of course, given my history of sexual abuse. I have struggled in my relationship with my father. When my memories first flooded back, I could barely tolerate sitting at the same table with him to inform him of my flashbacks and to hear him answer to them.

I learned first of his low level of personal accountability:

"We [family name] are all alcoholics, and we don't remember what we do when we're drunk."

After saying what I needed to say to him, I could not tolerate seeing him for a few years. I was too angry, too hurt. After much therapy and thought, I realized that my anger wasn't helping me. To the best of my knowledge, my father's molestation was limited just to me. My abuse stopped when my grandfather died and by the time my memories surfaced my father had retired from work and rarely left the house where he remains secluded under the care of a nurse's aid. If I had had any suspicion that he might have gone on to sexually abuse another victim, I would have done whatever I could to have stopped that from happening. Because there were no other victims at risk, I decided not to file charges.

I feel in my core that most people are basically good and decent but have the capacity to do awful things. Some people are sick and twisted and do horrendous things. I retain this faith in their basic humanity, not to excuse them or to deny the need to keep them from doing more damage, but because I believe that people have the capacity to change, even if ever so slightly.

My initial feelings of anger and hurt at learning what my father and grandfather had done to me evolved into sorrow for what happened to me. This shift in my attitude did not dismiss the importance of the ramifications of my sexual abuse in my mind. It did not stop me from getting the help I needed to heal the best I could. It did not stop me from speaking out to my family and friends about my sexual abuse. It did not stop me from being ultracareful about being victimized in other areas. But it did allow me to have more choices about how to deal with the relationships in my life. I chose to have limited, casual contact with my father. I discovered that I benefit from trying to understand what makes him do the things he does, to learn more about him so that I could learn more about myself. It was certainly healthier than choosing to hold onto my initial anger.

The shifts I had in my own reactions to my sexual abuse could be mirrored in the public's perception of how to handle sex offenders. When we get past the outrage, perhaps we may more clearly see our way into how to deal more effectively with the problem: how to treat criminals who have victimized children, how to help those who are beginning to become sexual predators, and how to empower our children so that they may become invulnerable to sexual abuse.

# CHAPTER TWENTY-SIX

*Amy:*
# Advice for Protecting Your Children

I once asked Alan what his greatest weapon was in his crusade to ensnare and abuse hundreds of children. He answered quickly and succinctly with one word—"listening."

It sounds so simple, but it is a profound answer. Listening is easy to do, and yet in practice, it is difficult enough for many people that it often does not occur. Our lives include so many responsibilities that in the few hours of contact that we have with our children, there is often little time for listening. There is work to be done, there are schedule demands, and there is always the television or computer screen competing for attention—ours and our children's. We must remember that we do have options to open communication channels. This protects our children from seeking an attentive listener elsewhere. I have found that one of the most viable mediums is one that most children already find engaging: music.

Rarely do I witness a child (or anyone for that matter) who does not respond readily and positively to music. Parents and caregivers can use this inherently powerful vehicle to deepen communication with children.

Ask to listen to your children's favorite music. Regardless of how you feel about this particular music, listen in an open, engaging way. You do not want them to feel that you are interested in it only to condemn it. This mere request will make your children feel recognized and important.

Whether you listen to it alone or with your children, listen intently, not just with your ears but also your mind and heart. Try to understand what it is about this music that engages them. You may disagree vehemently with the lyric message or the sound of this music, but regardless of your own feelings about it, it's their choice. It is not necessarily a mirror of their entire selves. Perhaps it is a reflection of their anger, wishes, or fears—complex or delicate feelings they could never express in words or act out—but the music does it for them.

As you listen, try to be aware of anything in this music that may reach you. Try not to say judgmental things, to your children or even to yourself. Keep your mind open. Envision it as a new food you are trying in a foreign country. You may very well not love it, but you set aside these reactions because you want to try something authentic from that land. Presumably you want to experience something new or you wouldn't have traveled there. Listening to your children's music is equivalent to visiting their land.

This music may make you recall music you loved as a youth but that your parents censored. (Remember the objections parents had in the 1960s to music of the Beatles and how tame that music seems today?) It may make you become acutely aware of your own fears for your child growing up in today's hard-edged society. It may make you angry that a certain level of promiscuity is not only allowed but also promoted. Allow your children's music to reach you, and then take time to reflect.

Before you share your own thoughts about this music, ask your guide (your children, the ones who brought you to this land) what their feelings are. Don't be surprised if the answer is a flippant "I dunno, I like the cover," or, "Nothing, it's just on the radio a lot."

This kind of response could be a manifestation of their feelings of trepidation. It can be very scary to share one's music with one's parent. Sharing music is often very intimate; it can be likened to sharing one's soul. Remember this, and listen reverently to whatever your children choose to share with you.

Then, ask if they would like to hear your reactions to the music. Honor their answer. If they say no, a possible response could be, "Okay, I'm glad I got to hear your music, and maybe sometime when you feel like it, I could tell you my take on it. Thanks for sharing it with me."

If your children are willing to hear from you, remember the analogy of the new foreign food. Although you may wish nothing more than to spit it out, you don't do so for fear of insulting the cook. On the other hand, you don't want to lie and say it's delicious if it's not (because then you'll be given more of it to eat). It's the opportunity of the experience itself that you are seeking and getting.

Find things about the music that reached you that can increase communication between the two of you. Show your openness to learn more about it: "I wonder what that singer was feeling when he was singing really loudly"; "I wish I could have understood more of the lyrics so I could understand the song even more." If there was something you genuinely liked, great—share that. But most of all, listen and accept that this music is part of your children.

This simple technique of listening to your children's

music must not be underestimated. It entails listening to, learning about, and accepting your children in a very real way on their own turf. But this technique need not be limited to music. Your children may be more interested in sports or fashion. Find what is appealing to them and become engaged in learning about those activities. Listen or you put your children at risk. Even if you feel great love for your children, which is certainly a key to being a good parent, you are not fulfilling your obligation to protect them unless you are an actively involved, open, and accepting parent.

Alan clearly outlines his techniques for capturing children emotionally. He even acknowledges the power of music as a manipulative tool. We need to be able to capture our own children the same way, for their health and safety.

Alan wrote: "I see if the desire, ability, and skill needed to communicate openly and fully with those around you is not developed in early childhood, the results are almost always going to be disastrous. The irony? That so much in life could either have been avoided, or at least corrected, simply by talking about it.

"I see this constantly, not just in my own life but also in the lives of the men surrounding me. The vast majority of the men here lived their lives surrounded by people who could, and often did, attempt to help them change the direction of their lives. But that critical communications link had not been forged in childhood, and as a result of that, they stayed tightly locked in their own internal hells, later to exchange those states for their current ones of incarceration.

"Music is a most intelligent and successful approach in reaching children, especially those locked within their own fears, insecurities, and confusion. It offers that all-important neutral ground, that small bit of safe territory in a world that appears much more like a minefield than a garden. I know that music, listening, and acceptance are keys to unlocking a child's private cell because I've used these same tools for destructive ends for so many years in the past. I used songs to entice children to open up to me, to tell me how they felt about their families. Then I used that information to bring them closer to me and further from their families. That barrier of silence that so many children lock themselves behind is not easily cracked, but once it is, the potential for changing the courses of their lives (either for the good or for the bad) is absolutely laid bare and ready for the taking.

"So, my friend, use it, knock down as many barriers as you can, and help the world learn something about the power of communication and the urgency for using that tool at the earliest possible age."

# CHAPTER TWENTY-SEVEN

*Amy:*

# Strategies for Better Communication

It's my belief that too many books and instructional materials available are only targeted to parents of kids *who have already been abused*. Obviously, those materials provide real help for families in trouble. The problem is too much of the available material has failed to address the more critical issue of *prevention*.

Since we can't be with our kids every minute of every day, how can we, as parents, raise the kind of child who will not be tempted by anything a potential abuser has to offer? I think if we take another look at Alan's history, as well as the history of nearly every other sexual offender with whom I've worked, we will find that their abuse strategies have some salient characteristics in common. These are having the ability to make a child feel worthwhile; having the means to make himself seem desirable; having a method of drawing the youngster into the abuse in such a way that the child feels there is no escape; and having a mask that keeps other adults from discovering his horrible secret.

When parents ask me, "How can I protect my child?" my

answers revolve around a central theme: communication. This may seem too general and too obvious, but I believe that parents can establish methods of communicating with their children that are unlike anything we have seen before in parenting. It's important to remember that until a generation ago or so, the conventional wisdom dictated that children were to be seen and not heard and that adults—any adults— are the ultimate authorities in a child's life.

This attitude has mercifully changed. But in many cases, our communication skills have not caught up to the concepts of modern parenting we find in books and current psychology. We know that we should talk to our kids, but we often don't know how. Still, we must be willing to learn and to take those first steps toward improving family communication. If we don't talk to our children, they in turn won't feel they are able to talk to us—especially about anything as terrifying and private as childhood sexual abuse.

All of this takes much time and effort, and an absent parent cannot do it. A parent must make communication a priority in order to be a vital part of his or her child's life in a meaningful way. The danger is that someone potentially destructive to your child will make this connection if you don't. Consider the depth of Alan's understanding of the importance of communication:

### Alan Speaks:

Saying "I love you" to a child who is totally convinced that you don't even know him, and that if you did, you could never love him, simply isn't enough. First, we need to make that child feel that he or she really is important to us and that what we love is all of them, including their bad parts, their fears, and their failures. Somehow, we need to begin to say I love *you* ... who you are ... not what you are. And we desperately need to learn that communication is only one part talking, followed by one part listening. I abused so many innocent children simply because I was willing to listen and to let them see my imperfections. I worked, continually, to give them a sense that I, for one, did not expect perfection from them. When something that they said was wrong, I tried to help them to correct their own error, rather than making a point of demonstrating their mistake.

I tried to create an environment in which they were free to speak of anything and not afraid of either not knowing or being wrong. In that simple bubble of acceptance, they felt very special. Tragically, I used this insight for a totally selfish and destructive end. But if I could make them feel special, why can't others learn to do the same for the betterment of these kids? And, what scares me most is that if this is not learned, there will always be more people like me out there offering a costly and devastating alternative.

I targeted victims who clearly showed that their communications network was failing them. I did this because I knew that in the pain and confusion of their abuse, they would have nowhere to turn for help. I knew that because I'd been there and stayed there. If parents can provide the same sounding board that I offered, then the children would have no possible need for the magic I sell. If a child feels accepted, respected, wanted, and listened to at home ... nothing I have to offer will prove appealing.

### Amy Responds:

I have outlined some concrete steps that can lay the groundwork for improved family communication: child empowerment; secrecy versus privacy; the open-door policy; ask and be told; pay attention; try to understand; and trust your gut.

## Child empowerment

Parenting styles have changed a great deal in the past few decades, and one of the areas where we see that change most evidently is child empowerment. Keep in mind that the element of control is central to the success of the would-be molester. Our task then, is to raise children who respect adult authority but are not slaves to that authority. If children feel confident saying no to adult authority figures, they are at considerably less risk for abuse. Psychologically, this means raising children with strong ego structures who will respect others *because they themselves are respected,* not children who obey out of fear or who hesitate to voice their opinions and concerns because they believe that as children, they will not be taken seriously.

For example, I remember knowing that my parish priest, Father Rudy Koss, in Dallas, Texas, was "doing things" to the boys in our congregation. As a young teenager, I was very active in the church, and as a victim of abuse myself, I sensed what was going on. But I was afraid to speak out; I felt that I would be disregarded and disbelieved if I even suggested that a well-respected clergyman would be capable of anything as horrendous as sexual abuse. So I kept quiet. Now, decades later, his victims have come forward to speak of the immense damage they suffered and continue to suffer at his hands. His victims have been awarded the greatest monetary judgment ever brought against the Catholic Church (at the time of this writing) prior to the current, ongoing scandals, and many have lost their spirituality, in addition to having ramifications of sexual abuse.

I bear the burden as an adult of having known what was going on: If only I had spoken up, what lives could have been changed? We hear of survivor's guilt in relation to atrocities such as concentration camps—what about survivor's guilt in the case of sexual abuse? I've spoken with female friends who have struggled with complex feelings upon learning that their fathers had singled out one of their sisters as a sexual abuse victim.

Obviously, they did not genuinely wish to have been included in the abuse. However, each one had spoken of a strange hurt that they felt at not having been the one chosen. Some of them stated that they felt undesirable and rejected, and others felt immense guilt because they could not protect their sisters. In addition, I have several male friends who also learned later in life that their sisters had been sexually abused, in most cases by the adult male figure in the family (father or stepfather). They experienced feelings of rage and guilt for not having known how to keep their sisters safe. Many of these friends, both male and female, recall sensing that something was awry in their homes, but they had neither the language nor the power to speak up and voice their concerns. Let's hope we can help our children's generation become better equipped to protect themselves and each other.

### Strategies

Perhaps the easiest way to raise children who trust their own opinions is to let them know early on that their opinions have real value. Give your children choices in their daily lives—what they want for dinner, what they wear to school, where the family goes on short trips. Even though many of these choices may seem inconsequential at the time, they serve to build a child's self-esteem as well as the sense that they exercise a degree of control over their own lives.

As long as he or she feels empowered in this way, as long as the natural impulse to exercise some control over his or her own life is not frustrated, an abuser cannot gain the first critical degree of control over your child that begins the abuse cycle. Remember Alan's history: He drew his victims into a false sense of intimacy in part because the children felt powerless at home. If your kids feel powerful about themselves, the abuser's brand of false friendship will hold little charm or attraction.

Don't disregard your children's reactions to certain situations. Talk about their feelings as well as your own. Foster empathy when and where you can. Teach your children to take action when they feel a situation calls for it, while at the same time allow them to know that actions have consequences.

Distinguish between assertiveness and aggression, certainly, but remember also that a child who truly respects authority is one who has been respected. Examine how you defend your child in public. When she or he is being attacked on the playground, what do you say or do? Do you remove yourself from the situation, hoping the children will resolve the situation among themselves? Do you remove your child from the playground? Or do you involve yourself in helping your child defend himself or herself appropriately?

When you witness an upsetting incident in a restaurant between another parent and his or her child, do you ignore it? Or do you discuss it with your child so that she or he can make sense of what is happening and perhaps be reassured that what they are witnessing would not be how your family would handle the situation?

As a child, I watched my mother become extremely angry in many stores. This was often understandable, depending on the ineptitude or rudeness of the sales personnel. Her method of coping was to walk silently out of the store without making her purchase.

Her anger was palpable and was often misdirected at us

on the way home. She was not able, or did not feel it worthwhile, to comment to the salesperson whose actions triggered her angry reaction. It was not surprising that she reacted this way to improper behavior in public since she dealt similarly with improper behavior at home. It is also no surprise that I go the other direction in public. If I feel I am being mistreated by store personnel, I immediately tell them what I feel is inappropriate about their actions. If I see no change in their behaviors, I summon a manager and report the offense.

My insistence on standing up for what I believe is right in such situations is not only limited to that which pertains to myself; sometimes it extends to others. If I witness a parent hitting a child in a store, I intervene. If I'm alone, I might ask if I can entertain the child for a few moments while the parent catches his or her breath. If I am with my children, I may explain to them (often in words loud enough to be heard by the angry adult) that the parent is angry at the child but needs to find other ways to express his or her frustration since hitting only teaches hitting.

My methods of reacting to situations that necessitate child empowerment arise from my own feelings of vulnerability as a child. I believe it is important that even those of us who grew up feeling strong inside examine our current methods of empowering ourselves and our children. Without this strength, our children are fragile. Would-be molesters are tuned into this fragility, and if they sense it they will use it.

### Secrecy versus privacy

As Alan's history (as well as my own) has shown us, secrecy is an essential element in the pedophile's system of abuse. Chronic abuse cannot be sustained without secrecy. It is your responsibility as a parent to remove that element of secrecy from your family life without destroying your child's sense of privacy. This can be a challenge because we all require some personal space.

Ask questions, but be willing to share your reasons for asking. Always let your child know that your desire to know details of their lives grows out of your fascination with them as individuals, not solely from the desire to be nosy or intrusive.

### Strategies

Let your children know that they can trust you. Demonstrate that you are able to keep their confidences, and always respect their desire for confidentiality, even if you don't entirely understand their reasons. Structure your confidences in such a way that avoids bargaining or bribery.

Obviously, it's unnecessary to burden your kids with inappropriate or sensitive information, but show your vulnerability and let them know that their opinions and input count. Contrary to what you might feel or believe, this kind of sharing does not make children become insecure about your ability to be a good parent. It actually strengthens children's understanding and respect to see that you are an imperfect human being who is desirous and capable of changing aspects of your behavior. Above all, stress the idea, whenever you can, that yours is not only a parent-child relationship but a person-to-person relationship, as well. You needn't compromise the boundaries of your role as parent and protector by being best friends with your kids, but you can let them know that they are respected people, celebrated as individuals with needs, thoughts, and opinions of their own.

### The Open Door Policy

Make sure that your home has an open-door policy. Encourage

the use of your home as a meeting place for your children's friends and a hub for all kinds of activities. Make sure you know whom your kids are hanging out with. Give yourself a chance to get to know these people—baby-sitters, scoutmasters, the leader of the church choir, etc. Don't assume that because your child is under adult supervision she or he is safe. Finally, have your child stay in a group environment for outings and field trips. There can truly be safety in numbers.

## Strategies

The open-door policy should apply to all family members. Try to ensure that there is interaction among all members of the family, including the adults. Invite your children to get to know your own friends and visitors, and pay close attention to your and their reactions to these encounters. Furthermore, encourage your children's analytical skills, and teach them to delve beyond appearances. Ask them how they feel about certain people or why they think a particular individual might have chosen to present himself in a certain way. Help your child to understand that people have motives that aren't always obvious. You needn't make them suspicious of others, but you can enable your child to see that everyone has needs and desires that govern their behaviors.

## Ask and Be Told

When your children return home (from school, lessons, trips, or other outings), ask what they did and how they felt. Note their reactions carefully, and follow up when things don't seem right or if their responses are unduly vague. Don't be satisfied with just the highlights. Request a detailed chronology, but always in the spirit of an engaged interest rather than a controlling inquisition.

Open-ended questions will yield much more communicative answers than yes-or-no questions, especially with your teenagers. Compare, "Did you have a good time at the party?" to "Tell me about the party." If you use the latter statement, you may learn about things you hadn't even considered.

## Strategies

Here again, you will encourage your child to be more communicative if you are forthcoming with details of your days, as well. Coax your kids to ask you questions: How was work? What happened at your meeting? Where did you go for lunch?

Talk openly about your feelings, and discuss your interactions with others. Although it can be a problem, especially for older children, to be open about their lives, your willingness to be forthcoming will in turn send the message that communication is not only welcome but also to some degree expected. If your child seems to resist or "can't remember" the details of his or her day, be patient. Get the ball rolling, draw them out by starting the process of sharing: "I remember I used to hate when...." or "My Little League coach was the yellingest man I ever knew."

If you have concerns that need to be voiced, do so in such a way that you don't alarm your child or provoke defensiveness. Start your discussion with phrases such as "I was wondering if...." and "It seems to me that...." Learn what your child responds best to and adapt your skills accordingly. Learn when your child is most likely to talk and make yourself available at those times. Even if they are less desirable times (such as in the car when you could be making calls on your cell phone, or late at night when you want to go to bed). Find the rhythm that inspires communication and follow it.

## Pay Attention

We need to remind ourselves to look at our children's bodies and listen to their feelings about them. Why does his head hurt before church each week? Why does she get a stomachache right before the baby-sitter arrives?

Don't assume the most likely, plausible, or convenient explanations for seemingly innocuous ailments. Really listen to your kids before dismissing their complaints. When I was a child, for example, I had that terrible psoriasis on my pubic area. My mother simply didn't realize it could be related to stress. And although she took me for medical treatment of the physical problem, she was too uninformed to be able to recognize the underlying cause of my condition.

## Strategies

Just as you must listen attentively to your children, you must also watch them carefully to try to pinpoint specific ailments and correlate a pattern, if there is one. It may be useful to ask your child to keep track of the conditions surrounding his or her own problems.

Sometimes the discovery that those headaches happen every time there is a soccer practice, for example, can lead to real solutions. Additionally, talk about your concerns with other adults whose experience and opinions you value. Trade war stories with other parents. Ask questions. "Did your Janie ever feel funny or sick when she went to piano lessons?" "How did your Bobby deal with it when he had all that detention last year?"

Finally, keep in mind that sometimes other people can see our kids more objectively and clearly than we. Solicit their opinions, and listen to what they have to say.

## Try To Understand

Alan made his victims believe that only he could understand them. We need to do whatever we can to prevent our children from feeling misunderstood, or they may seek outside validation from someone like Alan. It is difficult to understand someone else, especially one from a different generation. Our childhood experiences took place in a time and atmosphere that is totally foreign to the world our children live in today. In addition, our own expectations of and desires for our children cloud our view of them as the individuals they really are. As parents, we must be reflective as much as possible in our conversations if we are truly to understand our children.

## Strategies

As your child speaks of an upsetting situation, try phrases like "that must have been awful" or "I hear you saying _____" (repeating some key words or phrases). This helps the child feel that you are truly attentive and are getting the gist of the situation. Ask for clarification if you don't understand something, and do this in a gentle way: "I need help getting what you meant when you said she _____. What does that mean?"

This kind of reflective dialogue needs to continue long after the conversation has ended. We must constantly reflect on our parenting skills if we are to raise strong, safe, happy children. We need to look at what we have said and done at the end of each day and examine what propelled us to react.

Ask yourself specific questions like, "Do I encourage my children to stay out late with friends because I was a bookworm in my youth and regret not having been more social?" What wishes do we place on our children that were unrealized in our own childhoods? In order to understand our children, we need to understand ourselves first.

## Trust Your Gut

It's important to honor your intuition, even if you have a hard time accepting that anyone might possibly want to harm your child. I offer an example from my own experience. My mother acknowledges how uneasy she felt when my grandfather bought me baby-doll pajamas, and sat me on his lap to clip my toenails. But in that moment, she allowed herself to rationalize away her feelings of unease and discomfort. And the instant she did so, I was left unprotected.

## Strategies

Perhaps we can't do better than the old adage: Better safe than sorry. Apply it to all the relationships your child has with other people. You don't have to become hypervigilant or sever ties with anyone who makes you uncomfortable without apparent reason, but it does mean you must be cautious.

Don't leave your child alone with anyone who makes you uneasy, even if that person is a relative. If your child must interact with such people, turn your time together into a family time. Listen to your own feelings and watch your kids carefully before, during, and after such interactions. As parents, we can be forgiven for being overly cautious, but we will never forgive ourselves for failing to see a situation that, in many instances, was obvious from the start.

I cringe when I think about Alan's victims' parents driving them to the campsite. I can only imagine how they felt after learning what happened to their children. They, like my mother, did not know the dangers of the situation in which they were placing their children. Yet most, including my mother, did the best they could for their children. It just wasn't enough. Now we know better and have the obligation to improve the manner in which we protect our children.

# CHAPTER TWENTY-EIGHT

## *Alan:*

# Advice for Parents

Over the years I have witnessed Alan's desire to educate and protect children against people like himself who are not locked up. He recognizes the extreme damage that his actions have caused. Early in our music therapy sessions (more than a decade ago), he spoke of a letter that he wished he had been able to send to parents. I wrote his words down as he said them, in streams of phrases. His messages fall into three categories.

### To parents of children who have been molested

A typical initial response that parents have when they learn that their child has been sexually abused is disbelief. It is so overwhelming to think that their own vulnerable youngster could have been exposed to such an atrocity. Then feelings of anger often emerge—first and most obviously, anger toward the perpetrator, then anger at themselves for not having protected their child. Alan's thoughts for these parents were:

You've got a lot of work to do. Unfortunately somebody

has devastated your child, and you may not even see it yet.

And the child may reassure you that in fact, "Hey, I'm okay." But you've got to get help for him or her. Simply because children have been taught to say, "Hey, I'm okay," they have been taught *not* to discuss this. They have been taught very carefully to internalize the emotions that come with it.

"My child didn't come tell me what was going on." That child couldn't tell you what was going on, and *no*, he didn't have to be threatened. It's just that he participated in such a hideous activity, something that he knows innately is wrong, that he or she is just too embarrassed to come forward and talk about it.

He or she is going to need a lot of help. You are going to need a lot of help. And at the same time, you are going to have to be a big part of the help that your child receives. There isn't much that you alone can do for your child because you don't know what he or she has been through.

You might know the physical acts that have happened, but you do not have the training to know the extent of the damage that those physical acts have caused.

So the priorities right now should be that boy or girl. Your priorities right now should be seeing that while all the memories are very, very fresh and the pain is very, very real, you get the child to someone that she or he can relate to so that he or she can let out all that has happened.

### *Amy:* To parents of sexually dysfunctional children (children who may themselves become child perpetrators of younger children)

Sexual dysfunction in adulthood is clearly defined in many psychiatric textbooks and has to do with impaired sexual functioning. Defining sexual dysfunction in children is murky because children are not sexual beings in the way that adults are.

Terms such as premature ejaculation and functional vaginismus hold no meaning when applied to children, but children can be sexually dysfunctional for many reasons and can exhibit symptoms in just as many ways. A sexual dysfunction may be present if the child's behaviors contain elements of sexuality that a typical child would not have experienced or be concerned with, or if his or her sexuality is not at an age-appropriate level. A sexual dysfunction in a child is also defined by the pathological level of attention the child pays to his or her own sexuality.

A mild level of sexual dysfunction may result from witnessing sexual acts on screen or in real life. Seeing these acts may have been extremely upsetting to him, and he may feel too guilty to talk about it with his parents. He is left alone to deal with his feelings of uneasiness and lack of knowledge about what he saw. These feelings may cause him to behave in sexually aggressive ways toward girls and women in his environment for no apparent reason.

He may poke adults' buttocks or pull on their breasts. He may engage in sexualized play with his toys or with his body. While it is typical for a child or an adolescent to be extremely curious about his own body, as well as others, it is not normal for a youngster to show an interest that is aggressively or obsessively expressed.

A higher level of sexual dysfunction may exist in children who have had direct experiences. For example, a baby-sitter may molest a young child so often that this youngster becomes sexually aroused and begins to masturbate often and in public. This behavior shocks others, and the child is ostracized. Then this child finds solace in masturbating several times a day. While masturbation is a normal function, excessive masturbation—to the point of skin sores, irritations, and infections—is not.

The following story exemplifies a more severe form of sexual dysfunction, one that involves others. One of my music therapy patients was an eight-year-old boy who had been repeatedly sexually abused. He began sexually intimidating younger boys in the bathroom and reenacting his abuse in a ritualized way. He became obsessed with his sexuality. Even common events such as urinating became a sexual stimulus for him, and he eventually became incapable of attending to schoolwork after using the bathroom. In this case, an ordinary event, urinating, became sexualized in a child who had developed a sexual dysfunction. Such severity suggests a dysfunction so strong that the child may come to abuse other children.

The onset of sexual dysfunction can be triggered by seemingly innocuous things as well as by distressing events. Unless these children receive open, knowledgeable, and loving communication, there will be ramifications that can include an escalation into becoming sexual predators themselves. This communication must begin with the parents but must also involve mental health professionals. Immediate action is essential, not only for helping these children but also for protecting countless other children.

Alan wrote with great feeling about his own childhood and was able to think creatively about what might have prevented his behavior from taking shape and proliferating so destructively:

"If we can look for and deal with broken communications in young offenders, and in children who may not have offended but are at risk of slipping away, perhaps we can reach them, or rather help them to reach us, before they have faded so far into the darkness of distortion that the journey back is doubtful. If I could speak to the parents and adult providers of the world and tell them just one thing, it would unquestionably be to keep that binding element alive and healthy in their child 's life. Listen, and do everything within your power to keep that boy or girl feeling that, regardless of anything else that life may toss at them, they have one, solid, perpetual lifeline.

"I can think of nothing that would have penetrated my thick defensives more than a simple, honest, nonjudgmental assurance that I wasn't alone. Our country is filled with unnoticed, quiet, cutoff kids, many of whom are living in families who are blind to the communication shutdown, and sailing ahead as if life were squarely on course. If we are ever to have a serious impact on sexual abuse, I believe that it will begin by introducing a binding element into their young lives. If only we can find a way to get these kids to risk talking."

A caring parent who has a sexually dysfunctional child has huge obstacles in understanding the situation. Like parents of victims, they must withstand the impact of dealing with the knowledge that their child may have been sexually hurt. Then, on top of that, they must cope with the idea that this hurt has caused ongoing physical acts that are sexually atypical and perhaps quite destructive.

Alan's messages to parents of children in this category were:

They're not going to outgrow it. It's not a stage that they will pass through. And regardless of how you hate it, you've got to accept the fact your child has something that you can't handle alone and that you really can't help with.

You've got to find someone who can because the child is in no position to help anybody. The child is fighting with everything he has just to barely stay alive,

He's in a period where he just can't comprehend, and he can't look forward. He sees himself stagnating, and the only thing he really enjoys in life is what he's doing. It's the only thing that's really his. And pretty soon it changes from that which he *likes* to do to that which he *has* to do.

*He's hurt, he's hurt badly.*

He doesn't need to be taught elocution and tact and decorum, how to survive among adults. He needs to be taught how to survive among kids.

He needs you not to look at his potential but at his person, not to sit with expectation but to sit and talk. He needs you to create an environment where he could come to you, and tell you how hurt he really is.

*(Amy: This next portion seems to reflect Alan's anger at his own actions and at not having been stopped by others. Although we'll never know if he could have, in fact, been stopped, his rage is apparent in the following passage as well as the deflection of responsibility that may be sensed by the reader.)*

And if you let him go, you're guilty, you're guilty of destroying his life.

And in a way, you're guilty of all of the lives he will destroy.

And for what?

Simply because you didn't want to discuss something that was unpleasant? Simply because you didn't understand it?

You can't stop what you don't understand. You've still got to deal with it. You can't be the ostrich burying its head in the sand, because that kid is still there, still out there, going in circles, trying to figure out why you've got your head in the sand.

And the answer to that is pretty clear. Because you don't really care. And once he has that message, then you can't help him because like everybody else in life, he's put you into a category of people who don't really care.

That's the final category. That's when he says laws don't apply to me because I can't have anything else in life. Nobody comes, nobody's going to teach me what to do or when to do it. Then I'm going to play by my own rules.

**To parents of children who have not (yet) been molested**
*(Amy: Alan's messages to these parents underlines his belief that prevention is possible.)*

Provide an open dialogue between you and your children to the point that they feel that they can come in, discuss anything with no taboos. Let them know they'll get legitimate answers for their questions.

When you raise children like that, they cannot be molested short of physical rape. They certainly cannot be conned into chronic pedophilia for two reasons. You know with an open dialogue at home, they're going to go home and discuss this, and because the pedophile listens intently to what these children say.

If the pedophile picks up the message that your children can go home and communicate, the pedophile will back off. Those kids are the safest kids in the world.

So if you really want to protect your children, don't worry about a lot of peripheral things. The number one major item is *talk to them.*

# CHAPTER TWENTY-NINE

## *Amy:*

# Conclusion

The pedophile's greatest tool is listening, so that must be your greatest defense in protecting your children from sexual abuse. Communicate with them in an open and heartfelt manner every chance you get. Use every interaction as an opportunity to let your children know that you are interested in what they think and feel and that you accept them exactly as they are. The foundation of a strong bond between parent (or caregiver) and child can withstand much turbulence and many storms. It is essential against sexual predators.

We need to examine our communicating styles. As parents we need to be reflective and responsive, not reactive. This must happen in all areas of our lives, not just the ones we think pertain to our children's sexual education. True, it may be far easier to teach our children about sex in ways similar to how we were taught, but this age is far different from past eras. Our children will undoubtedly be exposed to far more sexualized material than we ever were. And although we may be uncomfortable discussing issues of sexuality with our children, be assured they desperately need guidance.

Sexual abuse is about many things, not just sex. And it's not as if bygone eras were ever able to protect children from sexual abuse. It happened then, it's happening now, but it does not need to continue. It's up to us to protect our youngsters.

Pedophilia is a sickening phenomena not cured by incarceration alone. Neither Alan nor I have the answer regarding how to "cure" the pedophile. We do know that the problem needs to be recognized, its devastating and escalating ramifications need to be acknowledged and questions regarding how we all are dealing with it need to be asked. What has been done thus far has *not* been effective. Megan's Law is proof of that. As each day passes more pedophiles enter our society.

In order to put a halt to the horrendous numbers of children sexually abused each day, we must finally be open to hearing the words that are hopefully still ringing in each reader's ears from Alan's voice. As parents and society we must tackle sexual abuse early and energetically. And we can only do this by listening and seeking information instead of by simply punishing and covering up.

Recall Alan's initial words to me, "If you want to understand me, listen to my music" and know that if we want to understand sexual abuse, we must listen closely to what this pedophile has to say. And we must learn to listen.

The last time I saw Alan was after he had been incarcerated for a decade. A television producer from a network show and I flew to the prison where Alan is currently incarcerated to discuss the plans for an upcoming show about our "story." Although we had corresponded by mail and phone during this period, I had not seen him for ten years. This, along with the fact that I was going to be away from my then-infant son made me more than a bit nervous.

I was eager to see with my own eyes how Alan had weathered his time in prison and where his spirit rested regarding his pedophilia. In just the few hours we were there it became strikingly and painfully clear that in spite of all of his intellect, insight, and desire to rehabilitate himself, he, and most notably, the system, had failed. As we were getting up from the table in the visiting room to say our goodbyes, Alan asked if we knew what time it was. We told him 2:30. Alan hesitated for a moment and looked out the window. With an affirming nod he replied "Yes...the children are just getting out of school now."

# *Suggested Readings*

Bass, E. & Thornton, L. *I Never Told Anyone.* Harper And Row, 1983.

Briggs, F. *From Victim to Offender: How Child Sexual Abuse Victims Become Offenders.* Allen & Unwin, 1995.

Carnes, P. *Out of the Shadows.* Compcare, 1983.

Carnes, P. *The Betrayal Bond.* Health Communications Inc., 1997.

Carnes, P., Delmonico, D.L., Griffin, E. *In the Shadows of the Net.* Hazelder, 2001.

Carter, Wm. L. *It Happened to Me: A Teen's Guide to Overcoming Sexual Abuse.* New Harbinger Publications Inc., 2002.

Castillo, R. *Not With My Child: Combating What Predators Do to Sexually Abuse and Silence Children.* United Youth Security, 1998.

Chase, T. *When Rabbit Howls.* Jove Books, 1987.

Colton, M. & Vanstone, M. *Betrayal of Trust: Sexual Abuse By Men Who Work With Children.* Free Assoc. Press, 1996.

Copeland, M. E. & Harris, M. *Healing the Trauma of Abuse*. Lightbourne Images, 2000.

Crewdson, J. *By Silence Betrayed: Sexual Abuse of Children In America*. Harper And Row, 1988

Danica, E. *Don't: A Woman's Word*. Cleis Press, 1988.

Driver, E. & Droisen, A. *Child Sexual Abuse*. New York Univ. Press, 1989.

Elliot, M. *Female Sexual Abuse of Children*. Guilford, 1994.

Engel, B. *The Right to Innocence: Healing the Trauma of Childhood Sexual Abuse*. Ivy Press, 1989.

Faller, K.C. *Child Sexual Abuse: In Interdisciplinary Manual For Diagnosis, Case Management And Treatment*. Columbia Univ. Press, 1988.

Farmer, S. *Adult Children of Abusive Parents*. Ballantine, 1989.

Forward, S. & Buck, C. *Betrayal of Innocence: Incest and Its Devastation*. Penguin, 1978.

Fraser, S. *My Father's House: A Memoir of Incest and of Healing*. Harper And Row, 1987.

Fredrickson, R. *Repressed Memories: A Journey To Recovery From Sexual Abuse*. Fireside, 1992.

Freyd, J.J. *Betrayal Trauma: The Logic of Forgetting Childhood Abuse*. Harvard Univ. Press, 1996.

Grubman-Black, S.D. *Broken Boys/Mending Men: Recovery From Childhood Sexual Abuse*. Ivy Press, 1990.

Harrison, K. *The Kiss: A Memoir*. Random House, 1997.

Herman, J.L. *Trauma and Recovery*. Basic Books, 1992.

Hunter, M. *Abused Boys: The Neglected Victims of Sexual Abuse*. Fawcett Columbine, 1990.

Kelly, L. *Surviving Sexual Violence*. Minnesota Univ. Press, 1988.

# Suggested Readings

Lew, M. *Victims No Longer: Men Recovering From Incest and Other Sexual Child Abuse*. Nevraumont, 1988.

Maltz, W. *The Sexual Healing Journey: A Guide For Survivors of Sexual Abuse*. Harper Collins, 1991.

Miller, M.S. *No Visible Wounds*. Fawcett Columbine, 1995.

Petersen, B. *Dancing With Daddy: A Childhood Lost and a Life Regained*. Bantam, 1991.

Poston, C. & Lison, K. *Reclaiming Our Lives: Hope For Adult Survivors of Incest*. Little, Brown & Co., 1989.

Pryor, D. W. *Unspeakable Acts: Why Men Sexually Abuse Children*. New York Univ. Press, 1996.

Renvoize, J. 1982 *Incest: A Family Pattern*. Routledge & Kegan Paul, 1996.

Russell, D. E. *The Secret Trauma: Incest In the Lives of Girls and Women*. Basic Books, 1986.

Ryan, M. *Secret Life: An Autobiography*. Vintage Books, 1995.

Sankin,D. J. *Wounded Boys, Heroic Men*. Adams Medic Corp., 1998.

Shengold, L. *Soul Murder: The Effects of Childhood Abuse and Deprivation*. Fawcett Columbine, 1989.

Silverman, S. W. *Because I Remember Terror, Father, I Remember You*. Univ. Of Georgia Press, 1999.

Spring, J. *Cry Hard And Swim: The Story of an Incest Survivor*. Virago Press, 1987.

Tschirhart-Sanford, L. *The Silent Children: A Parent's Guide to the Prevention of Child Sexual Abuse*. McGraw-Hill, 1980.

Ward, E. *Father Daughter Rape*. The Women's Press, 1984.